Lazar:
The Autobiography
of My Father

Lazar:
The Autobiography
of My Father

ખ

by Leonard Yanow
and *my*

ખ

The Viking Press · New York

B
Yan

To Flo

LIBRARY OF CONGRESS CATALOGING IN PUBLICATION DATA
Yanow, Leonard, 1903–
Lazar: the autobiography of my father.
Includes bibliographical references.
1. Yanow, Leonard, 1903–   2. Jews in Poland—
Biography.   3. European War, 1914–1918—Personal
narratives, Jewish.   4. Poland—Biography.   I. my,
joint author.   II. Title.
DS135.P63Y36   947'.652 [B]   79-22624
ISBN 0-670-14231-X

Printed in the United States of America
Set in CRT Gael

Maps by Paul J. Pugliese, GCI

The over-all number of minds is just one. I venture to call it indestructible since it has a peculiar time-table, namely mind is always *now*. There is really no before and after for mind. There is only a now that includes memories and expectations. But I grant that our language is not adequate to express this, and I also grant, should anyone wish to state it, that I am now talking religion, not science—a religion, however, not opposed to science, but supported by what disinterested scientific research has brought to the fore.

—*Erwin Schrödinger*

We cannot, however, speak of a direction for time as a whole, but only for certain segments in which relatively isolated ("branch") systems undergo thermodynamic changes. For some segments (those in which processes may occur in such a way that entropy decreases), we shall have to recognize the peculiar possibility of a reversal in time direction.

—*J. J. C. Smart*

Preface

1. ל

How can I explain. I close my eyes and I am my father, a boy of seven in Volkovysk. My father was seven years old twenty-nine years before I was and yet I know his seven as I do my own. I just close my eyes and I'm there . . .

Mother is at the wood stove cooking potato soup, Father is in bed reading the Gemara, Frumke is at the table peeling onions (dear Frumke!) and Schmuel is on the floor playing with Rosetka. I am just coming in with an armful of wood for the stove . . .

I see all this very clearly, see it, hear it, smell it, and yet they are *his* mother and father, *his* sister and brother, *his* dog. Somehow I am able to go back again without ever having been there before.

2. ♪

She blurted it all out as fast as she could so that I wouldn't have time to be alarmed, and she tried not to sound frightened herself, but fear was in my mother's voice. And when I got to the hospital and managed to see him for the few minutes each hour that they allow in Intensive Care, plugged into monitors, tubes running from his nose and arms, his pale blue eyes fluttered open and he smiled weakly and I could see he was frightened too.

I wanted to tell him that it was all right, that I loved him, that I didn't have the feeling he was going to die, but it isn't easy to discuss feelings with my father. I held his hand instead.

He closed his eyes and drifted off for another hour.

3. ♪

He had been staring across the room for almost an hour. His eyes were on me, but he seemed somewhere else. Valium. I sat by the window, warming in the sun, and watched the monitor over his head, the lines and peaks moving regularly across the screen, white on gray. He was in a private room now, out of the woods and on his way back.

The tracings on the monitor were repetitive. Suddenly a line grew longer and there was an extra peak and I was jarred into remembering it was my father's heartbeat on that screen! I looked down at his face, expecting pained distortion. But he was still staring at me as before.

Finally, without changing expression, he spoke, and I realized he hadn't been somewhere else, only thinking.

"You write about all those people. Why don't you write

about me? I'm as interesting as they are."

It wasn't a question. He was asking me to write about him, god knows how long it had been on his mind. Knowing him, quite a while. Now he had had a heart attack and he wasn't going to wait any longer to ask. Still it took him an hour to get it out. My father hates to ask anybody to do anything for him. He would rather endure.

4. ੫

In her fear of being left alone, Mother now hovered over him as though he were sick and fragile. He went along with it because he too was still frightened, though of course he told me he was not afraid to die. But he was recovering anyway, and after several months he came to accept the possibility that angina might not keep him at death's door after all.

He wouldn't let go of the idea that I should write about his life and he raised the subject at every opportunity. He had decided it should be a book, a best-seller that would make me a great deal of money. Since he had always wanted to leave my brother and me a business or at least a lot of money when he died, and he had neither, the story of his life was all he had to leave me. A best-seller would be his legacy.

I wanted him to write it himself. The man had no hobbies, nothing to do that was his own now that he was retiring and moving to Florida. He would need something to replace his work, something to give him pride and a sense of accomplishment. Moreover, the two of them were already together too much of the time and it was beginning to show. Without work, there would be no space between them at all. Writing about his life would give him something to do alone and would serve to get her out for a few hours a day too. It would be good therapy for them both.

I didn't tell him that, I said I was too busy. I told him that I was working on a new book and on two magazine articles and it would be impossible for me to start another project for at least a year. I told him he should do it himself, that his stories were very interesting and that if he didn't write them down no one was ever going to hear them. His response was: You're the writer, not me.

My father and I are equally tenacious, but we finally compromised: he would write and I would edit. It was the only arrangement I could think of that would get him started. I was living in Maine then and we arranged that he would mail his writing to me as he went along. No timetable was set. I agreed to edit the notes, but I made no commitment as to what I would then do with them. It's your story, I told him, not mine. I didn't know then how mistaken I was.

5. ৮

When the first batch of notes arrived, they were typewritten on eight-and-a-half-by-eleven bond and the style was very affected. I smiled. The collusion was obvious, my father doesn't type and he doesn't read Harold Robbins.

I confronted them on the phone and he complained your mother doesn't think anybody will be interested in this and says I shouldn't include that and besides I can't spell and I'm no writer. And she said I only helped him a little that's all.

I explained to them both that writing is solitary work and it was very important for him to do this alone. I told her to play golf with her friends or take a course in something or even write a book of her own, but to stay out of his. Then I told him that he was too a writer. Don't worry about spelling or punctuation, I said, that's what editors are for.

As I hung up the phone, it occurred to me that I had just become an editor.

6. ↲

The notes were now coming on six-by-nine lined notebook paper, handwritten on one side, a dozen pages or so every few weeks. The last page often ended in mid-sentence. He sent the originals, he kept no copies.

I had never seen my father's handwriting. Letters were always written by my mother. The only thing I ever saw was his signature on my high school report cards, only the good ones, and it became a sort of badge of honor. I still get a warm feeling when I see it, neat and orderly like him, yet with a flourish at the end as he would be if he could. My father is a stiff and formal man; he doesn't want to be but he is, and he has always had great trouble showing his feelings. This was like receiving personal letters from him to me and I cherished the intimacy. It was something I had little of from him as a boy.

From the age of five until I left home for the army and surprised him with an embrace, the only physical contact that I remember between us was when my legs hurt so badly from playing that I couldn't sleep and he rubbed them with alcohol. Men don't kiss, he told me when I was a boy, they shake hands. But I idolized him. I loved to work with him around the house or in the garden, and then to hear him tell my mother what a good worker I was, just like he was when he was a boy.

He was awkward at sports and embarrassed by his awkwardness, so we didn't play together as sons and fathers do. We did go deep-sea fishing once, off the New Jersey shore, with the men in his office, but he kept me awake all night with his snoring and I was seasick the whole next day. It was not a very successful outing.

He was, however, a superb horseman and an excellent instructor and that we did do together nearly every Sunday. Riding side by side, horses at a brisk trot, doing my best to imitate his straight back and a post that barely left the saddle, boots shined, stirrups long to allow a standing canter, toed in, both hands on the reins, knees firm, up, down, up, down ... there was good rhythm between us when we rode together, or when we worked together, a closeness that was nonverbal. On those occasions, his awkwardness and inhibition were gone, replaced by the quiet confidence of knowing exactly what he was doing and doing it well.

The rest of the time, he deferred to my mother and we never talked about what was inside. As we grew older, our politics diverged. He became more conservative, I more radical. Discussions deteriorated into arguments, arguments led to silence. We loved each other, but we had less and less in common. It troubled us both for many years that we had so little understanding of each other.

My writing brought us closer again. It seemed to help him understand me. Now his writing was helping me to understand him. Some of his stories were familiar to me, having heard snatches of them as a child, but the rest were new and I found myself reading with genuine fascination of the life and adventures of this small boy who would one day be my father. The handwriting was large and clear, but his spelling was phonetic and the punctuation was irregular. He had very little formal education, none after the age of eleven, and like most immigrants in those days, he taught himself to read, write and speak English when he arrived in America. It couldn't have been easy.

This is not easy, he kept reminding me. I gave him as much encouragement as I could, because I didn't want

him to stop writing, but I still had no idea what to do with
his notes. He was growing impatient, kept asking me what
I intended to do with them, and I was constantly looking
for new ways to stall.

Six months went by. A year. I had moved to California
and was now living on my boat in Santa Cruz. Gradually, I
became immersed in my father's life in Russia. My words
of encouragement were now as much in my self-interest as
in his. I began to pressure him to write more regularly and
he resisted, saying what difference did it make if I wasn't
doing anything with it anyway. It was my turn to grow impatient. When the last page would break off in the middle
of a story, as it did when he was raped by a German soldier, I could hardly contain myself until the next manila
envelope would arrive with the rest of the story.

Yet, the stories were curiously devoid of feelings. It was
like a building with steel girders and no walls. His memory
was incredible. Names, dates, places, times, even the color
of eyes and hair and what kind of clothing was worn on a
certain day. But even in the most dramatic moments,
there were no emotions. He remembered the facts, but
not the feelings. If I pressed him on the phone or in letters,
asking him to describe how he felt during a particularly
emotional incident, his reply was that he could only do it
the way he was doing it, because he was no writer. You're
the writer, you'll have to make something out of it, he
would say. I could see it was going to be a problem.

7. ४

"I'm leaving for America soon," he said one day. "When I
get there I'm going to stop writing. This is very hard for
me. You don't know what it does to me, to have to go
through all this again. It looks like you're not going to do

anything with it anyway, so why should I keep writing?"

My father had been writing his notes for a year and a half. There had been two more trips to Intensive Care, both of them more scare than attack, which is the way it usually is with angina, but my father is a pessimistic fatalist. He had reached the limits of his indulgence.

But I was ready now. I knew at last what to do with his notes. For almost two years I had been studying and writing about autohypnosis and age regression, experimenting on myself with various techniques for revivifying memory. While my father had been writing to me about his childhood, I had succeeded in reexperiencing my own. I viewed this as a kind of time travel, speculating that beyond the three dimensions of everyday reality lies a dimension in which each of us is his own time machine. Why not use the same techniques to relive *his* childhood as I had my own, with his notes serving as cues?

For the last two months his notes had contained stories he had never told before, and yet they were somehow familiar to me. One story broke off in the middle and I had to wait for the next batch of notes. Instead, I closed my eyes and went there. I was my father, Lazar, in Volkovysk, and I finished what he was now writing about sixty years later. When the envelope arrived containing the second half of the story, it was as I had seen it.

Even his handwriting was becoming as easy and familiar to me as my own, and yet it didn't resemble the way I write at all. Once, I picked up a pen and tried to imitate his writing. I wrote my name on a piece of paper. It looked exactly like his handwriting. *The name on the paper was Lazar Unovitch!*

I approach this with an open mind. We have a narrow filter through which we construct the illusion of one reality. It is a useful but artificial constraint. Setting aside the filter permits the flow of many realities, too many, however, to grasp intellectually. But there is a *knowing* that transcends intellect, that is beyond conscious experience, and it is at that level of knowing that I am my father. It is there that space and time are not separate, there that energy and matter are interchangeable, there that everything is connected.

There is another possibility, less metaphysical, not contradictory but on a different level. I could have received my father's memory, genetically coded in the DNA and passed on at my conception, and that memory might now be distributed in the neural synapses of my brain. This apparent regression could simply be the accessing of stored holographic images.

Either way . . . mind or brain, or both . . . what I now had was a way to add walls to his steel girders. Using his notes as cues, I would reexperience some of the critical events and fill in the missing feelings. Of course, I didn't tell that to my father, I just said:

"Okay, I'll make you a deal. You don't stop. You keep writing, at least until the age of my conception, you don't have to go further than that if you don't want to. You do that and I'll start working on the book."

"Done."

Chapter One

1. צ

My name was Lazar Unovitch. I was born on the sixth of January 1903 in the small city of Volkovysk, under the Russian flag in the western state of Grodna Gobernin near the Russian-Polish border. I was the youngest of eleven children. Mother gave birth every two years.

The firstborn was Yitzak who died from tuberculosis at nineteen. I don't know anything else about him. Then came Benel, Kale, Label, Bashe, Yankel, Minoche, Motel, Frumke, Schmuel, and me.

My father's name was Dovid. He was five feet nine inches tall, weighed one hundred and forty pounds and had a thirty-two-inch waist. His hair was gray, almost white, slightly bald on top, and he had a gray beard down to the middle of his chest. His eyes were dark and he had a beautiful nose. My father seldom dressed in a full suit. Mostly he wore just pants, a shirt, an arba kanphot with a vest over it, a yarmulke, and bedroom slippers.

As far back as I can remember, my father was in poor health and rarely went out. He complained of headaches and stomach pains. Our family doctor said my father had *shlepoya kishka*, which means blind intestines, but he never really diagnosed the illness and we could not afford to take my father to a specialist in a big city.

My mother's name was Golde. She was five feet two and weighed one hundred and forty pounds. She had gray hair, blue eyes, and a round beautiful face, but she always looked worried and was seldom happy. She wore her hair in a bun, with a sheitel and then with a kerchief over it, but when she let her hair down to comb it, it was very long. She wore long dark dresses with long sleeves, usually with an apron. In the summer she rolled the sleeves up. She took the apron off for company.

We lived in a wood frame house, which was next to a two-story brick building which my parents owned and helped build about 1890. The brick building had three apartments, two on the lower floor and one on the upper floor. My parents rented the apartments out for income. Our wooden house had one bedroom for my parents with twin beds and one window, a living room with three windows, and a kitchen which was also part bedroom with one window and a wood-burning stove with a large oven faced with white tile. We used a lot of wood every year.

The buildings had no electricity, no water or bathrooms. We had a well outside. The barn was right next to the house and the outhouses were next to the barn. Winter came at the beginning of September and the snow and ice didn't melt until after Easter. Then everyone would chop the ice around their property and haul it away with the many feet of snow that had piled up all winter.

Our city had about thirty thousand people, including a large Jewish community. There was quite a bit of anti-Semitism, but the pogroms were in the big cities far away and we got along with our Gentile neighbors. The local police were wined, dined, and bribed by the Jewish merchants, and they kept order in our city, so it was only the youngsters who fought every Saturday night and no one was hurt badly by the stones that were thrown by both sides.

Volkovysk was about five or six square miles. Most of the houses were wooden with red tin roofs. During the night, when people were asleep, the peasants would empty the outhouses and haul the waste away to use as fertilizer in the fields. The odor was so strong that it would wake you up, but to the peasant it was just another job. The peasants were very hardworking. Their own acreage was enough to feed them and their livestock, but they were always anxious to hire out for a few extra rubles. The women and children went barefoot even in the winter.

Our streets were paved with cobblestones and we had cement sidewalks throughout the city. The streets were kept clean, except for the horse manure which had to be swept up by the individual homeowner or shopkeeper. The main street was about fifty feet wide. In the center of town we had a big Russian Orthodox church with a lot of ground around it enclosed with an iron fence. The seating capacity was about four hundred and the place was filled every Sunday and holiday. There were also a number of smaller churches throughout the city, and the Polish people had their own huge Catholic church. You could hear church bells ringing everywhere on Sundays.

Across from the Russian Orthodox church was the one and only hotel. It had forty rooms and was very nicely furnished, with a huge bar on one side of the lobby and a dining room next to the bar with white linen tablecloths and napkins on the tables. The chairs in the lobby were covered with red leather and the wooden floors were highly polished. In the back was a big stable for the horses and carriages.

Our house was only a block away from the hotel, so whenever I had time I would stay in front of the hotel and sometimes people would ask me to take their horse and carriage to the stable or their luggage to their room, and I would get a few kopecks to buy ice cream. I enjoyed watching the guests arrive. Most of them were the high brass from the army post with their girls, and their beautiful horses and carriages were driven by their orderlies. Sometimes the rich landowners would arrive with their best horses to show off. They rarely came with their wives. Our city had plenty of whorehouses with lots of beautiful girls. In fact, there was one three blocks from my house.

In the winter it was twenty to thirty below zero with plenty of snow and ice, and it was dark from five in the afternoon until six-thirty in the morning, so the nights were long with nothing to do except for sitting around the table with a hot samovar boiling. Guests would drink hot tea in the hotel dining room. A great amount of vodka was consumed also, while people sat around getting acquainted and exchanging stories to pass the time away. Sometimes fights erupted, police would be called, arguments settled, and guests carried to their rooms. If they were not guests, they were carried to the street. None was arrested. The next morning all was well and quiet again and the place was ready for another day of business.

Four blocks from the hotel was the public market. It faced two streets, peasants drove in from either side, and it was on top of a hill, so horses had quite a time pulling their loads to the market. Three times a week, peasants from surrounding villages would converge on the market, bringing their livestock and produce to sell. Most of the merchants had their stores all around the market. In the center were a well and trough to water the livestock. At the far end of the market were several booths owned by the local bakers, who would sell fresh bread and rolls. You never tasted anything so good as a piece of fresh rye bread, especially with raw salt herring and a glass of hot tea.

At the end of the market days, peasants would congregate in the taverns on the outskirts of town, where they would buy herring and tea to go with their own bread and meat. They would also buy vodka and get drunk. I remem-

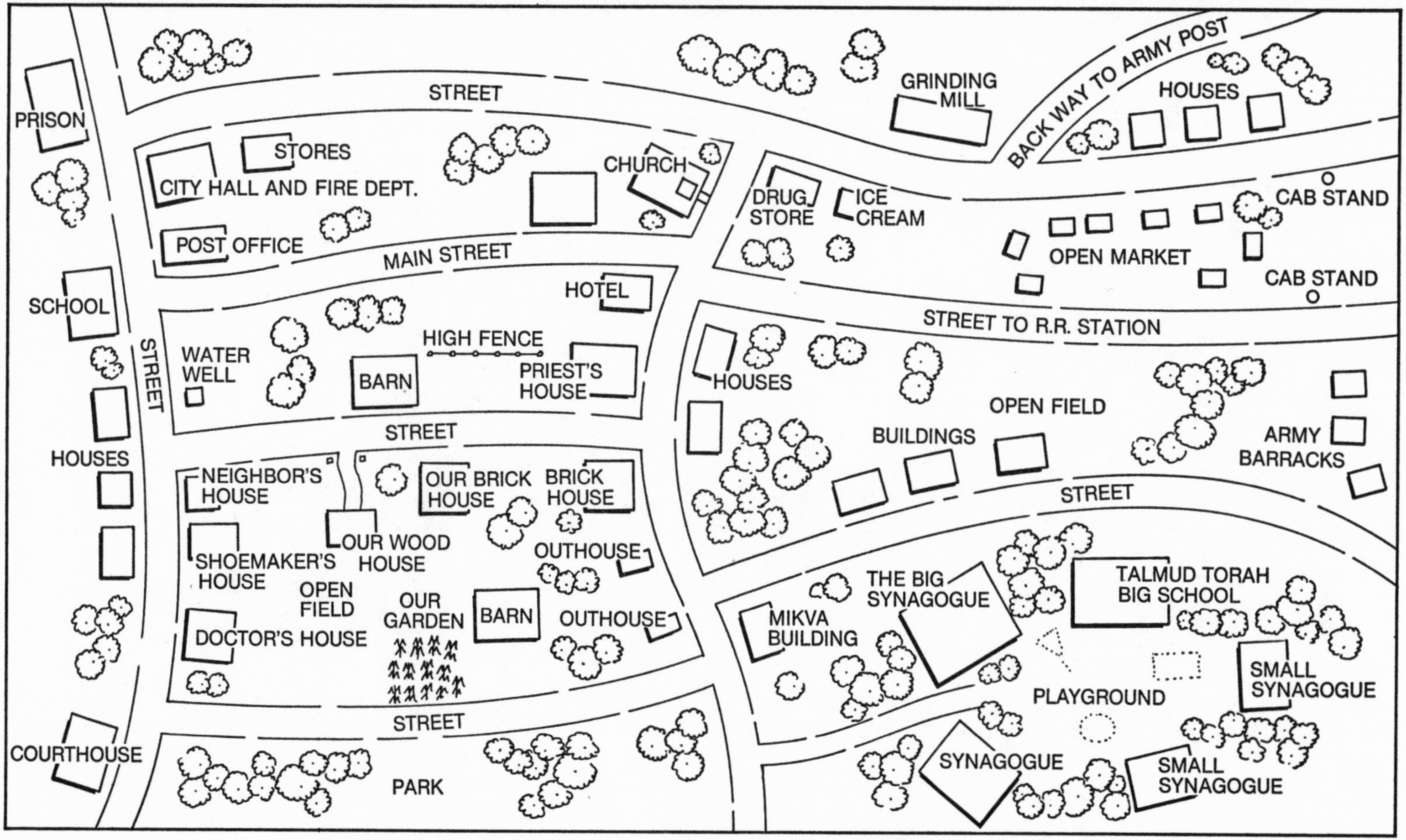
PRISON
STREET
STORES
CITY HALL AND FIRE DEPT.
POST OFFICE
MAIN STREET
CHURCH
GRINDING MILL
BACK WAY TO ARMY POST
HOUSES
DRUG STORE
ICE CREAM
CAB STAND
OPEN MARKET
CAB STAND
SCHOOL
STREET
HOTEL
WATER WELL
HIGH FENCE
BARN
PRIEST'S HOUSE
STREET TO R.R. STATION
HOUSES
OPEN FIELD
BUILDINGS
ARMY BARRACKS
HOUSES
STREET
NEIGHBOR'S HOUSE
OUR BRICK HOUSE
BRICK HOUSE
STREET
SHOEMAKER'S HOUSE
OUR WOOD HOUSE
OUTHOUSE
OPEN FIELD
OUR GARDEN
BARN
OUTHOUSE
DOCTOR'S HOUSE
THE BIG SYNAGOGUE
TALMUD TORAH BIG SCHOOL
MIKVA BUILDING
SMALL SYNAGOGUE
PLAYGROUND
STREET
COURTHOUSE
PARK
SYNAGOGUE
SMALL SYNAGOGUE

ber helping my uncle at his inn sometimes. I waited on customers and then helped them into their wagons, where they would fall flat on their faces and let their horses find the way home. I can still remember the smell of all the animals and the people in my uncle's smoke-filled inn.

My sisters and brothers were all gone from home by the time I was five, all but Schmuel and Frumke. Two went to France and the rest went to America where they heard there was gold in the streets. Mother cried a lot about her children leaving and going so far away. My father said America was *tref* because people worked on the Sabbath and he would never go there.

My father was originally in the wholesale-retail fruit business. Every spring he would travel to the big orchards and bid on their fruit for that summer, estimating the size of the crop from the number of blossoms on the trees. His estimate was usually very close to the yield. On July 15 he hired a watchman to prevent pilfering by the local peasants, and later in the summer he moved in for the two months before harvesting, living in the hut the watchman built. They did their cooking outdoors and took turns guarding the orchard at night.

When the fruit was harvested, it was stored in rented cellars and sold by my parents during the winter. My sister and I helped. My father's twin brother and two other brothers and their father before them were all in the same line of business. But when my father grew too weak to manage the fruit business, he decided that since he was confined to the house, we would go into the cigarette business by making cigarettes at home.

My mother became adept at blending the different types of tobacco. We bought the papers with the cork tip. My sister also learned to make the cigarettes, which we sold in boxes of one hundred. I was the clipper of the ends, the delivery boy, and the runner of errands. The quality of our merchandise became known even to the army and the high brass at the army post gave us large orders. We were the only cigarette makers in Volkovysk. Between that and the rents coming in from the three apartments, we were able to manage well for quite a while. In this way my father felt that by making cigarettes at home he was taking care of his family.

I loved my father very much, but I couldn't discuss personal matters with him. He was always sick and Mother was very careful that he shouldn't be aggravated in any way. She made all the decisions and was both mother and father to me. Father was a very pious and kind man and he was loved by all. He would sit at home all day, praying and learning. He had an excellent memory. He studied continuously in the Gemara, of which he owned a complete set, and he was also well versed in the Talmud.

Father often debated the laws with other learned Jews and he usually won, proving his point by bringing out the proper book. Until he grew too weak, he and I went to synagogue every Friday night and invariably he would bring home to dinner one or two poor men who were traveling through town. He would say if there wasn't enough food they could have his share, but Mother always managed to have enough.

2. ♪

One day when I was seven, I was attending morning services in the synagogue and we heard of a tragedy that had occurred in a village eight miles away. A Jewish couple in their seventies who owned a country store had been brutally murdered. They were the only Jewish people living among the peasants in that village. They had lived and traded with their neighbors in peaceful harmony for many years, until that one night . . .

"Lazar, did you hear? Two Jews were killed last night, chopped into pieces by a Pole! We're going there right after services. Want to come?"

It was the middle of the haftorah and services would be over soon. Lazar was sitting in the back of the synagogue with four of his friends. They were whispering to each other about the murder. Like the others, Lazar was curious and excited, but he hesitated about going with them to the village because it would make him late getting home.

"I don't know," he whispered back, "I have to go right home, my mother will worry if I'm late."

"But we're going to run all the way and then get a ride back with one of the peasant wagons coming to market. Come on, don't be a baby, we're all going."

Lazar was the youngest and was rarely included by the older boys. This was his first chance to do something big with them. "All right," he whispered excitedly, "I'll go!"

And they did run most of the way, shedding their jackets after the first half mile and tying them around their waists, hot and sweaty, grimy from the dust of the road, mouths dry and chests burning, shouting back and forth in nervous excitement to spur each other on, until at last they reached the crest of the hill leading into the village. They had slowed to a walk going up the hill, but the sight of the village below gave them new energy and they trotted down the hill, silent now except for their own heavy breathing.

The village was small, a tight cluster of thirty or forty log cabins with straw roofs. The dirt road on which the boys had come was the only road through the village, and it ran a straight line in one end and out the other, disap-

pearing into the woods beyond. Near the center of the village was the country store, a two-room frame house with the store in the front room and a back room where the old couple had lived. It was set slightly apart from the cabins around it and Lazar could see there was a crowd of people gathered in the front yard.

As the other boys jumped up and down in the rear of the crowd, straining to see over the heads of the peasants, Lazar pushed his way through to the front. He was hot and tired, his Sabbath clothes were streaked with dirt and he was sure to be late getting home, but he was at least going to see what was what for his trouble!

The constable, a tall and bulky man with a full black handlebar mustache and dressed in an ill-fitting tunic with baggy pants tucked into high black boots, stood on the steps of the store facing the crowd, his bulk filling the open doorway behind him. Near him, sitting on a rock, looking bewildered and making no move to escape, was the murderer, a lean gaunt young man in his mid-twenties with deep-set eyes and thin lips pressed tightly together. The constable was addressing the crowd.

". . . and he told them he wanted to buy some tobacco. It was late and they were closed, but they let him in because they knew him from buying in the store before. When he got inside, he says he hit the old Jew over the head with an ax, killing him instantly. Then the wife came in and saw what happened, and she screamed and he did the same thing to her. Then he says he brought in a log and chopped them up to bits on it." The crowd gasped. Lazar felt his heart pounding. "He says he doesn't know why he did it," the constable continued, "but look at him, friends. Obviously the fellow is mad!"

All heads turned from the constable to the man sitting on the rock. The man's eyes darted from face to face, as though fearing attack. For a moment his eyes were directly on Lazar, and Lazar, full of curiosity, stared back, but then they shifted to the man next to him and Lazar turned once again to the constable who was finishing his speech.

". . . So I'll take him to the city jail now. Let them worry about what to do with him. Oh, this is a terrible thing that has happened in our village, my friends, a terrible thing."

Lazar knew it was a terrible thing all right, but he still hadn't seen anything, only the crowd of peasants and the constable talking and the man sitting on the rock. He edged to one side, trying to see behind the constable, and as he did the constable shifted position too, moving closer to his prisoner, and now Lazar could see through the open doorway into the store.

There were several men moving about inside. They appeared to be cleaning the room or something; it took Lazar a few minutes to realize what it was they were doing. Then he saw it, the short thick log and the hacked-up bloodied pieces of the old couple. He moved slowly toward the house as the men put the pieces of bodies into sacks and carried them out to the wagon. He stared wide-eyed at the blood-stained floor and a single gnarled hand lying on the floor next to the log.

His stomach began to feel peculiar and his head light. There was a ringing in his ears. The constable's voice sounded very distant, like an echo, as Lazar continued to move closer to the house, staring at the hand, his mouth open and strangely dry.

"Boy! Come away from there!"

It was the constable. Lazar suddenly realized that he was no longer standing at the edge of the crowd, but was now well in front of them and nearly at the steps. The constable, knocking his curved pipe on the bottom of his boot and preparing to leave with his prisoner, was shouting at Lazar. Everyone was looking at him. Embarrassed, Lazar turned and ran quickly back to his friends.

The crowd was beginning to drift away in twos and threes, the excitement over, and the boys began to look for a ride home. Lazar turned once more toward the doorway. The hand was no longer on the floor.

. . . The funeral was held in our city and everyone turned out for it, Jew and peasant alike. A month later I saw him being led in chains to the courthouse for trial. This incident remains with me to this day. I regret having ever witnessed such a gruesome event.

3.

In 1912, I got a job in a clothing store, dusting suits and running errands for one ruble a week. I enjoyed my work and was happy to be able to help at home with my money. One day I was sent to a fur store to buy a fur piece for a man's coat which was being made at the store. I was told by my boss to pay for it and he gave me thirteen rubles, but he also said to try to bargain and get it for twelve and a half. I did as he told me and got it for the twelve and a half, but on the way back I met my cousin Gail.

When she heard the story, she decided we should buy ice cream with the money and I should tell my boss I had to pay the thirteen rubles. There was money left after we bought the ice cream, so she told me to buy a small purse and tell my mother I found the purse with the money in it. What I didn't know was that my boss had already arranged for the fur piece at twelve-fifty and was just testing me.

When I told him the lie, he fired me and I had to tell my parents the reason. My brother Label gave me such a whacking I couldn't sit down for a long time. It was a lesson I never forgot and I have never taken another penny for the rest of my life. I decided my father's preaching of "honesty is the best policy" was the only way to live one's life.

Schmuel played with fellows older than himself and would beat me up when I kept following them. I was always crying. Finally the family thought it would be best to separate us. My mother wrote to my brothers and sisters in America to send for Schmuel, which they did. After he left, my father decided I should leave Hebrew school and go to the yeshiva, which was in another city that took all night by horse and wagon to get to.

Mother made the trip with me and we went to a relative there. They agreed to house me, but were too poor to feed me. It was the custom for yeshiva students to be given meals by the townspeople, and my mother spent a few days rounding up seven families to feed me, one day a week each, for the year.

As my mother was getting ready to leave with the hired wagon, I realized I was about to be alone. I started to cry. I said I wouldn't stay, I would run away. My mother hadn't liked the idea in the first place, especially with only me and Frumke left, so she changed her mind and took me back home with her, and once again I was back in Hebrew school.

Our family doctor had a Gentile son-in-law who was principal of a one-room public school for boys. Jewish boys were not permitted to enroll in public school, but I wanted very much to learn to read and write Russian. One day when I delivered the principal's order of cigarettes, I pleaded with him to use his influence to get me in and he promised he would try. Two weeks later I was accepted. At age ten, I was the only Jewish boy in the school.

4. ₺

It was hell on earth. Especially at recess time when they would throw small stones and rotten fruit at me and call me *parchaty Zhid* (Jew with sores). I always sat alone, as they would not play with me. My friend the principal, who was also the teacher, was very kind to me. One day he noticed I was crying and he asked me what was the matter, but I didn't tell him anything because I was afraid they would gang up on me and that things would only get worse.

I was no longer going to Hebrew school every day and my father was very unhappy. However, I went to Talmud Torah every Saturday and Sunday afternoon and evening, and I studied with him whenever he had time, and my mother persuaded him to let me continue in public school. I didn't tell them about the trouble I was having with the boys in school. I was determined to stick it out long enough to learn to read and write Russian . . .

It was time for recess. Lazar dreaded recess. To avoid confrontation, he deliberately came to school earlier in the morning and managed to leave later in the afternoon than everybody else, but there was no way to avoid them at recess. Many times he wished he could ask his friend the principal for permission to remain inside during recess, but he knew that would only lead to questions he was in no position to answer.

Each day was the same. As recess approached, the class would become restless, anticipating play. The older boys would begin to exchange glances, looking pointedly at Lazar and back at each other, grinning. When recess came, they were always the first ones out, and by the time Lazar walked slowly through the doorway, they would be wait-

ing for him in the schoolyard, grinning. He was their daily sport.

Lazar was not afraid, yet he never fought back. It was complicated. Jews were not supposed to be in Russian schools. His friend the principal had obtained special permission for Lazar to attend the school, but if there was trouble the principal himself might get into hot water with his superiors and Lazar might be told to leave. Father was sick. The family depended on Lazar now. If he could learn to read and write Russian, instead of just Hebrew and Yiddish like everybody else, he would be able to earn more money for the family. It was important, therefore, not to make trouble.

If a Jew gets beat up, there is no trouble; but if a Jew fights back, that is trouble. So Lazar never fought back. He took their insults and their punches and he never complained. Sometimes, when he couldn't hold back the tears any longer, he would find a corner somewhere and cry. But always alone, never in front of them. He couldn't understand why they hated him so, why they wouldn't let him play with them and be their friend. There was nobody he could even talk to about it. It was simply one more thing he had to keep locked up inside him.

As Lazar came out of school that day, he knew what to expect. Most of the class had split up into small groups, running, playing tag, throwing balls to each other, but four of the older boys were standing off to the side, facing the door. As usual, they were waiting for Lazar. Trying to ignore them, he walked slowly to the other side of the small schoolyard and sat down on the old tree stump, his back to them. He could feel them watching him. One laughed and said to the others:

"It looks like the Jew doesn't feel like playing again today. Hey, parchaty Zhid, what's the matter, too good to come over here and play with us, or are you afraid?"

"Maybe he doesn't like us!"

14

"Well don't get too close to him, you could catch something. He has all those sores under his clothes. It comes from drinking blood."

"Ha, ha! Hey, Jew, is it true? Do you drink blood? Hey, stinking Jew, turn around, I'm talking to you!"

They laughed and threw dirt at Lazar. Little pieces of sand and rock stung him on the back of the neck. He could feel the anger and hurt and frustration welling up inside him and he fought back the tears. Oh, why wouldn't they just let him alone? Suddenly something soft and wet hit him behind the left ear, hit him hard and splashed, and as his hand went instinctively to his head, he smelled the sour rot of overripe tomato. Tears came to his eyes as he heard their laughter.

But abruptly, the laughter stopped and Lazar heard another voice say, "Don't do that anymore. The Jew does nothing to you. Leave him alone."

Lazar peeked over his shoulder. It was the big Polish boy, the one who always stood apart from the others, the one they called Gregori. He was holding one of the boys by the wrist with one hand. It must have been the one who had thrown the tomato. The boy was squirming, trying to break Gregori's hold on his wrist. The laughs had turned to frowns as the Russian boys considered this unexpected interruption in their daily sport.

"Hey, what's it to you, Gregori? Since when do you love Jews?"

"Don't do that anymore, understand?" said the Polish boy, ignoring the insult. "Or else."

He released his grip, turned, and walked over to Lazar. He put one hand on Lazar's shoulder and asked, loud enough for the others to hear, "Are you all right, Lazar Unovitch?"

Lazar answered shyly, yes, all right. He was as stunned as the Russians by this unexpected turn. Gregori had never spoken to him, not one word. He was surprised Gregori

15

even knew his name. Now, after watching them pick on Lazar every day for three weeks, Gregori had suddenly come to his defense. It was a miracle!

He was overwhelmed. Just when everything had seemed so hopeless, to have a friend, a protector, he was so happy and proud that somebody cared, that somebody understood that he meant no one harm, wanted only to be friends, wanted only to have somebody to talk to, to play with . . . but in his shyness, he couldn't tell this to Gregori. He could only look up at this blond Polish boy who was the same age as he but stood a head taller and smile at him through his tears.

Recess was over. Lazar and Gregori walked together, past the four Russian boys now silent and glowering, and entered the school.

. . . Gregori fought many a battle for me. In school the kids called him a Jew-lover, but he didn't seem to mind. He was a very strong boy and they were all afraid of him. As time went by, life at school became much easier. The two of us became real friends. I helped him with his homework, because schoolwork was much easier for me than for him, and I shared my school lunches with him.

His father worked in a livery stable, driving their coaches, and the family was very poor. Gregori stayed in our house, slept in my bed, and we did our homework together. He helped me with my chores around my house and I helped him with his at his house. We both helped his father groom the horses and clean the stables, and sometimes we exercised the horses. It was there that I learned to love horses. I wanted a horse of my own very much, but of course that was out of the question. We just couldn't afford it. It was all we could do to feed ourselves, let alone a horse.

At the end of the year we both passed to the next grade

at another school. The second school was a half-hour walk from home on the north side of town. Two doors away from the school was a *bardak* (whorehouse) which we all watched with great interest. Sometimes we could catch glimpses of the naked girls through the windows. They did a thriving business with the soldiers who were stationed nearby. Occasionally they would entice one of the older boys inside and then the rest of us would tease him and joke about it for weeks.

One day the *bardak* burned down, taking the school with it. The volunteer fire department arrived too late and the whole block burned to the ground. They set up classes in a church and that's when my father put his foot down. No son of his was going to a Russian school in a church! That was the end of my Russian schooling after a year and a half, but I had learned to read and write Russian, so I was satisfied. And I went back to Hebrew school, so my father was satisfied too.

Chapter Two

1. ۇ

Volkovysk had a huge military post consisting of two branches of the service, infantry and artillery. Several thousand men and horses were stationed there. The soldiers lived in two-story brick buildings, alongside of which were huge stables for the horses and artillery. Married officers lived in single homes and bachelor officers lived in a separate building.

The ballroom was the most beautiful building I have ever seen. It had highly polished wooden floors with great crystal chandeliers hanging from the ceilings, each with hundreds of candles. Tables and leather chairs surrounded the dance floor and the tables were covered with white linens and set with the finest china, crystal glasses, and sterling silverware.

I used to deliver cigarette orders to the brass and to some of the single officers. I therefore had access to their homes and clubs and got very friendly with their orderlies. Sometimes I would give them a few cigarettes and they would show me around when there was nobody home. The Commanding Officer was a general.

One day when I delivered the General's order of cigarettes, I met his son, a young officer who had just graduated from military academy. His name was Alexi Gregorovitch. He was twenty years old, about six feet three, dark and handsome. He told me to tell my father that our cigarettes were very good and he would tell the other young officers to buy them too. As a result, our business at the post went up and I made deliveries almost every day.

On Sunday mornings a company of soldiers with a big band, led by a young officer on horseback, would march to the Russian Orthodox church for services. The brass would arrive in carriages driven by their orderlies. Just before church let out, the owner of the hotel would put chairs out in front for the C.O. and his staff. When services were over, the soldiers would form behind the church, march around the block to the main street and pass in review before the General.

After the parade, the General and his staff would go into the hotel for refreshments. No one else was allowed to go inside the hotel until they would leave. The whole town turned out for these Sunday parades and watched the General's son leading the soldiers on his handsome black horse. I waved to him once, but he paid me no attention. However, the next time he saw me in his house he explained that he had seen me but was not allowed to wave back when he was passing in review with his troops. He was very nice to me and I liked him very much.

A few months later, tragedy struck the General's house. The orderly told me the story: A ball had been given in honor of the newest young officers, including Alexi Gregorovitch. This was an annual affair, attended by all the high brass and their wives and daughters. There was much eating and drinking, everything of the best, and some of the officers would have too much to drink. Their orderlies would have to take them to their quarters, but no one was ever reprimanded because very often the C.O. and his staff were in the same condition.

The right-hand man of the C.O. was also a general and he had a beautiful young daughter who was very popular with all the young officers, especially with Alexi who was in love with her. I saw them together once and they were really a handsome couple. The night of the ball, she was dancing with another officer, and Alexi, who had had too much to drink, became very jealous. When they danced by him, he reached out and lifted her dress high in the air. Laughter broke out and she was so embarrassed that she ran from the ballroom crying.

Alexi's father came over and told him that he was under arrest, and then they took him out. The officer with whom she was dancing would ordinarily have demanded satisfaction, but since Alexi was the Commanding General's son, he decided to stay out of it. However, the girl's father demanded a court-martial within three days. The trial was set for the third day, and in the meantime Alexi was relieved of all duties and confined to his home.

He had no excuse for his behavior and realized that he had not only shamed the girl he loved, but had disgraced himself and his family. To go through with the court-martial would mean being stripped of his rank and uniform and dismissal from the army, an even greater disgrace, especially to his father as Commanding Officer of the post. On the second day, as the General and his wife were sitting down to dinner, they heard a shot from Alexi's bedroom. They rushed to his room and found their only son dead.

When the funeral was held at the big church, the whole town turned out. Alexi had been very popular. The girl left home and went to live with grandparents in Moscow. Three months later the General died of a broken heart. He was in his early fifties. Mrs. Gregorovitch became very ill and went to live with her parents in another city. The girl's father became the new Commanding Officer.

A big shakeup took place in Headquarters. Many officers

were transferred elsewhere and a new staff was formed. This had a big effect on my family, because we lost our best cigarette customers. The new C.O. was very strict and I was unable to make contacts with the new officers. At the same time, we lost several other good customers, including my friend the principal who was transferred to another town. Things didn't look good at all.

2. ʔ

Mother was worried. The cigarette business was continuing to fall off. One of our rooms was empty and less rent money was coming in. One of my father's brothers had a bad year in the fruit business and lost all his money. Naturally, my father told my uncle to move into our empty apartment with his family and to share whatever we had until he could get on his feet again. Instead of four, we were now eight.

Somehow Mother managed. She cried a lot, but never in front of my father because she didn't want to aggravate his condition. She did the best she could. She baked bread and made borscht and potato soup. We raised our own chickens and geese, so there were always eggs and a chicken for Sabbath dinner. Butter and milk we bought from our neighbors who were farmers.

Mother did her best to keep us happy. I know that all families think their mother is the best, but let me tell you, in my opinion there was no other woman like her!

I decided to enter an apprenticeship in watchmaking and repairing. There was one jewelry store in Volkovysk. Two of my brothers had learned the trade there before they went to America and the owner knew me from when I used to bring my brothers their lunch. He gave me a job cleaning the store and running errands, and at the same time I learned the trade. My father was very unhappy that he was the man of the house and unable to support his family, while I, a boy of eleven who should have been in Hebrew school, was out working. But there wasn't much he could do and we needed the money, so he decided that it must be God's will.

The first thing I learned to work on was alarm clocks. I learned to take them apart, clean them, and put them back together again. After six months on my job, the boss called me to the front of the store one day and gave me a raise. He said that he was pleased with the way I was doing my job and now that I could work on alarm clocks I was entitled to more money. I felt very proud of myself. I was now making three rubles a week and that meant we could buy meat a couple times a week for dinner.

Meanwhile, my mother had the idea to rent the vacant lot behind our house, about two acres, and grow vegetables. She got one of our Polish neighbors to plow it up and she and Frumke did most of the work. I helped out after the store closed and on Sundays. The soil was rich and the yield was good and Mother had no problems selling the whole crop, except for what she canned for us for the winter. That gave us enough money to put a new shingle roof on our house and barn.

I never saw my mother work so hard. She wouldn't let Frumke carry anything heavy. Instead, she would load up her apron full of vegetables which she would bring in to clean before selling them. With my mother and sister working so hard in the garden, they couldn't help my father with the cigarettes, so we decided to give up that business.

One day when I came to work, my friend Joe who also worked in the store told me that his father was going to sell a few cows to raise some money. I got the idea that we should buy one. I came home all excited and told my parents about it. We had the new roof on the barn and plenty of cuttings from the vegetables and in the summer we could ask our neighbor the farmer to take our cow to pasture with his cows. We talked to our neighbor and he said it would be all right as long as we paid his boy a little something each week for looking after our cow. So my parents agreed to buy one.

The next week Joe's father brought us a young cow that he said would give us a lot of milk. Because I was his son's friend, he agreed to take what money we had and let us pay off the rest. He also told us if the cow was not everything he said it was, he would take it back and give us another, but it turned out to be a good cow and we loved her very much . . .

Lazar was very busy. Summer was drawing to a close and there was much to be done before winter came. Every morning before work, he milked Belka the Cow and walked her next door to join the other cows for pasture. Then he worked all day in the jewelry store, cleaning the floor, dusting the counters, running errands and repairing alarm clocks. On Mondays he walked two miles to the army post to check the clocks in the barracks, since his boss had a contract to service them, and often he would have to carry one or two of them back to the store for repairs. It was hard work.

When he came home from the store, he helped Mother and Frumke with the garden, picking ripe vegetables and bringing them into the house for cleaning or canning. By this time, Belka was in from the field and needed milking again. With winter coming, a loft was needed in the barn to store hay and feed for the cow. Lazar bought boards and laid a floor on the rafters. Once a week he borrowed the neighbor's horse and wagon to haul Belka's manure, which he spread on the neighbor's field.

Firewood had to be bought at the market, and hay for

the loft, and the windows had to be stuffed around the edges to keep the cold winter winds out. By the end of the day, Lazar was tired and it was all he could do to just crawl into bed, curl up with Rosetka, and go to sleep.

Let me tell you, I didn't mind it a bit because I used to love that kind of work. However, between my job in the jewelry store and the work at home, I was very busy and there was no time to play, which was at this point far from my mind, and because of my father's illness I had to be the man of the house at eleven years old. I felt good about it because I loved my parents very much. By nature I was not lazy and I was willing to do anything to help.

I remember when I was a little boy my mother would take me into bed with her to sleep, and I used to cuddle to her and feel very secure. And when I would get sick with some child's sickness, my father would sit at my bed all night long to comfort me and walk the floor with me. One does not forget such things, and now it was my turn to do for them. Many nights now I lay awake and think of my dear parents and my life with them in Volkovysk. How I wish they were here now so I could continue to help them and what a comfort that would be. However, all good bad or indifferent, it must come to an end and your whole life is like a dream. We are here today and gone tomorrow. Yet, when you dream of your parents, what a comfort it is, it makes you feel that they are near you.

But even the man of the house has to have somebody to talk to, somebody to play with when nobody's looking, somebody to be a little boy with once in a while. Lazar had Belka and Rosetka.

"Belka, you were a bad girl today, you kicked the pail

over when Mother was milking you! Are you trying to cause trouble for me? Don't you know we need your milk to sell and for butter and cheese for Father? Do you think we can afford all this nice hay for you if you keep kicking over pails of milk? Do you?"

"Moooo!"

Lazar laughed. It seemed Belka was laughing too and having fun with him. Rosetka barked and shared the joke. Lazar put down the pitchfork, walked over to Belka, frowned and wagged his finger in her face in mock anger.

"It's not funny! This is verrry serious business, you silly cow, and just because Rosetka is laughing too is no reason for you to think this is a joke! You'd better never do that again if you know what's good for you!"

"Moooo!"

But he couldn't keep a straight face, not with Belka nuzzling him with her soft downy nose. He threw his arms around her neck and hugged her tightly. Rosetka, the little black-and-white terrier, jumped up on his leg, barked, then ran twice around the small barn as fast as she could and came back to jump up on his leg again. Oh, it was so good to be with his friends in the barn! He was surely a lucky boy to have Belka and Rosetka.

With one arm still around Belka, Lazar reached down with his other hand to scratch Rosetka behind her ears where she loved to be scratched, and she whined with pleasure.

"Don't worry, Rosetka, I love you too. I will always love you and we will be together forever, all three of us, eh, Belka?"

Belka responded with another long Moooo! and then turned her head toward Lazar and ran the flat of her tongue right across his face from ear to ear in a wet rough kiss.

"Aggghhh!"

ᘺ

... By the fifteenth of September, the garden was finished. Belka would still go to pasture until snow was on the
ground. We got the farmer to turn the ground over before
the first frost and when the ground was frozen I was able
to spread the cow manure around for next summer's garden. The hard work was over until next spring. As for myself, I continued to work at the store, but I was not too
happy there as I did most of the dirty work and the old
man did not try to teach me how to work on the small
watches. He said I was too young for it.

He concentrated instead on my friend Joe because Joe
was crippled and this was going to be his life's work. I
didn't feel bad about that though, because Joe was my
friend.

There were three of us working in the back of the store
... the old watchmaker, Joe, and me. Joe was eighteen and
very good-looking, but he had no friends because he was a
cripple. His left leg was shorter than the right one, with
the foot curved outward, and it just hung there as though it
had no life at all. His right leg was straight and he could
support himself on it with the help of crutches.

Joe lived on a farm with his parents about two miles
from Volkovysk and he came to work every day in a wagon
pulled by his dapple-gray pony, Tzyganka, which means
Gypsy. In wintertime he came in a sleigh. Joseph's father
ran the farm with the help of five Russian peasant families,
which he provided with food and shelter in addition to
paying them wages. He had a large herd of milking cows
and also owned a mill to which peasants from surrounding
villages came to grind their wheat.

Joe and I became very friendly and many times he
would invite me to his home for the weekend since we did
not work on Sabbath or on Sunday. I loved going to the
farm. There was always a lot of good food and I liked work-

ing on the farm and, although Joe couldn't get around too well on crutches, he was able to ride a horse and we often rode bareback around the farm.

So when the old man said I was too young to learn watchmaking and concentrated on teaching Joe instead, I didn't mind as there wasn't much else Joe could do because of his leg. But I wasn't happy with the job, just being an errand boy after school and now and then working on an alarm clock. I would have quit except we really needed the three rubles a week and I didn't know where else to go to earn money. I was still too young for most jobs.

3. ק

My mother never complained to us about her health. Usually if she was sick she would never even tell us. But she worked very hard that first summer in the garden and she started to complain of pain in her stomach. As time went by it grew worse and we finally made her go to our family doctor, Dr. Weiner.

The news was not good. Dr. Weiner said she had to have an operation. Since our little hospital had limited facilities, he wanted her to go to Warsaw to be operated on in a big hospital by a friend of his who was a very good surgeon. Mother couldn't make up her mind what to do, so she decided to ask the Rabbi for advice.

We had one rabbi in Volkovysk and nobody did anything without his advice. We all looked up to him as being next to God. There were six neighborhood synagogues and one big one which was near the Talmud Torah Hebrew school. The Rabbi was in the big one. I used to love to go on Saturday afternoon to hear him give a sermon.

When Mother went to the Rabbi, he told her that she should go to Warsaw and not to be afraid, that she would come out of it for the better. My father was pleased with the Rabbi's advice, but felt badly, more than he would let us believe, because he couldn't go with her. Frumke wanted to go, but Mother wouldn't hear of it. She told Frumke she had to stay home to look after Father and me, to take care of the house and Belka the Cow.

Before she left for Warsaw, Mother wrote to my brothers and sisters in America asking for money because we didn't have enough for the operation. But mail was very slow to and from America so we had to borrow from my uncles and our tenants. The following week Mother left by train for Warsaw. Two days later she was operated on and, sure enough, it was a tumor. The surgeon wrote Dr. Weiner and he came over to the house with the good news that the operation was successful and Mother would be fine.

The next week I told Frumke to take the train and go see Mother. Father agreed and Frumke went to Warsaw for a few days. I took care of the house and Father.

Lazar welcomed the chance to take care of Father, it was an excuse to be near him. Ever since Mother had gone to Warsaw, Father had gotten weaker and stayed in bed most of the time, reading or just staring out the window. It frightened Lazar. It was always so hard to know what to talk about with Father anyway, and when he was like this Lazar grew even more timid than usual.

Probably Father was still worried about Mother, and if Father was worried, Lazar thought, that was reason enough for him to be worried too. Every night, Lazar prayed to God that his mother would be well again and come home soon; and then he would cry himself to sleep, muffling the sound into his pillow or Rosetka so Father wouldn't hear him. It wasn't that he still missed snuggling up to Mother in her bed, he was a man now, after all, and no longer a little boy, it was just that he missed her, that's all. It was the first time she had ever been away, and with Father sick and Frumke away too, he just wanted his mother to be home!

I cooked. Not as good as my mother or Frumke but I managed.

I had trouble with Belka. She had grown used to Mother or Frumke milking her. She would look at me and Mooo! as if to say: I don't want you to milk me. I didn't know what to do, so I got our neighbor's wife to come over and milk her until Frumke came back.

Three weeks passed and then Mother came home. She was very weak but happy to be home again. And so were we all. Thank God! Frumke took good care of her and wouldn't let her do anything around the house. Father took on new life with Mother home again, we all did. And more good news, a few days after Mother came home we received a money order from my brothers and sisters and a whole case of kosher meat in cans! The meat was just what Mother needed to get back her strength and the money enabled us to pay back my uncles and our tenants for what we had borrowed.

A few months after the operation, Mother at last felt like her old self again and took over the reins. We had our "ruler" again and we were all happy about that. Passover was approaching and as my mother was getting ready for the holidays, another great surprise, my sister Minoche (who had changed her name to Mina in America) came with her little daughter for a visit! At eighteen Mina had been the first to go to America, and when she married her husband Joe, who was in the building trade, she sent for each of my brothers and sisters, one by one, and she and her husband let them stay in their house until they were able to establish themselves.

Mina's main reason for coming was to see if she could

29

talk us into going back with her to America. That's all she talked about, but my father was stubborn. He still wouldn't hear of it! Mother went to the Rabbi for advice. His answer was not to go against Father's wishes. So once again the decision was that the four of us should remain in Volkovysk.

My sister and her daughter went home at the end of six weeks and I cried because I didn't know if I would ever see her and my cute little niece again. America seemed a long way off then. But spring was here and there wasn't much time to think of America, there was a lot of work to be done. I finally quit my job so I could work in the garden and help Mother.

Now Belka decided that she wanted to be a mother, and I had to take her to my friend Joe's farm as they had a bull. Luckily I only had to do this once; sometimes you have to take them several times. About then little Rosetka disappeared for a whole day and before long it became pretty obvious that she too was going to be a mother.

It was a busy summer, but a profitable one. The garden was even more successful than the first year and we made good money from it. That fall, Belka gave birth to a calf and Rosetka had four pups. We gave three of the puppies away and kept the fourth. The calf, however, was not up to our expectations and we sold it at the market the following spring.

4. ל

In our Jewish community we had a small theater located on the second floor of a large building which was owned by a Jewish furrier and during the winter, when people had more time for entertainment, Yiddish plays were staged using local talent. The director of these plays was a young woman and she was very good at it. She was getting ready to put on a musical comedy, *Koldunia,* in which there was a scene calling for a boy of my age who could sing. I decided to try out for the role.

At the tryouts I was the only boy with an alto voice and I got the part. The scene took place in a market and I had to carry a tray of hot buns and sing a solo telling people that these were the best buns you could buy and nowhere else can you get them as good. In the other scenes I sang in the chorus. For some reason I wasn't shy at all on stage and I must say I was pretty good. My family had never heard me sing before, except in prayers on the holidays, and when Mother and Frumke came to see the play they were very proud of me. The play was a big success and ran for several nights.

In the chorus with me was a girl named Chanka who also did a solo dance in the play. She was a year older but about two inches shorter than me and kind of cute, with a round face and long dark-brown hair. I had not met her before because she lived on the far side of town and because girls didn't go to Hebrew school together with boys. I liked her a lot.

One night after the show, I took her for ice cream and then walked her home. She told me I was the first boy who ever took her to an ice cream parlor and walked her home. Her parents knew mine. They had a small grocery story in their neighborhood . . .

"Is that you, Layshka?"

"Yes, Mother."

"Come into our bedroom, Layshka."

It was late. Lazar had tried to come in quietly so as not to disturb his parents, but his mother was a light sleeper and heard every little sound in the night. He tiptoed past

Frumke who was sound asleep and peered into the darkness of his parents' bedroom, his eyes gradually adjusting until he could make out the outline of his parents. They were both sitting up in bed.

"Yes, Mother?"

"Why are you so late getting home from the play?"

Lazar was still feeling elated. After all, he had sung well in the play and the audience had applauded the solo, and he had had his first "date" with a girl! It had been quite a night. So there was excitement in his voice when he answered, though of course he tried to sound very nonchalant and mature.

"Oh, well, I took Chanka for some ice cream after the play and it was late so I walked her home too and you know they live all the way on the other side of town. You shouldn't have worried, I'm not a baby anymore."

"The boy is too young to be buying girls ice cream already," his father said in a low voice to his mother. "He should be thinking about learning the Talmud instead of thinking of girls."

"Now, Dovid," said his mother, "there is no harm in having ice cream with a girl and walking her home so she doesn't have to be alone at night, it is perfectly natural. Chanka is a nice young girl and her parents are good people. Layshka, you go to sleep now, there is work in the morning. And next time, you should think a little more of your mother and father, worrying about you until all hours of the night. Next time, ask before. Now go to sleep."

"Yes, Mother. Good night, Mother. Good night, Father."

Lazar quickly undressed in the dark, humming softly his solo in the play, and got into bed. Then he hugged Rosetka, kissed her twice and whispered, "Good night, Chanka!" But Rosetka didn't know what that was all about and merely squirmed away to curl up at his feet and go back to sleep.

꙳

... I didn't see Chanka again until spring. Frumke and I were walking one Saturday afternoon, about a mile out of town along the railroad track, where everybody walked to a little park that had tables and benches and where you could also buy ice cream and cold drinks. I spotted Chanka walking with her brother Aaron who was fourteen. I waved and they came over and sat with us. I was very glad to see her, although Frumke didn't care much for Aaron because he was younger than she was and very shy.

We had some ice cream and then we walked home together, and on the way I told them about the pigeons I was raising up in our loft. I started with four and then they had six young ones, so I had ten. We rarely used the loft in the house, except when it rained and Mother hung up the wash to dry, so I had cut a small hole in the wall, built a little platform outside on which they could land and take off, and then I screened in a section of the loft so they couldn't fly all over it. I put straw down on the floor, which I changed when it got dirty, and I fed them once a day with oats and cooked potatoes and vegetables.

Chanka and Aaron wanted to see my pigeons, so on the way back from the park they stopped at my house and we all went up to the loft. Aaron was excited and said he would ask his father if he could raise pigeons and would I then help him to build a coop like mine? I said I would, of course, because in back of my mind was the idea that it would give me an excuse to see his sister more often. But, as luck would have it, his father said no and I didn't get to see Chanka again until one day early in the summer when she surprised me with a visit.

Her excuse was that she had come to see the pigeons. Mother and Frumke were in the garden weeding. Father was taking a nap. We went up the outside ladder into the

loft, but the pigeons were all out flying around somewhere.
Chanka didn't seem too disappointed . . .

*They both seemed to have the same idea and it had very
little to do with pigeons. They sat down on the floor next to
each other, neither one saying a word, and stared blankly
at the empty pigeon coop. Suddenly Lazar had an over-
whelming impulse, he didn't even have time to think
about it, he just twisted around, grabbed Chanka into his
arms and kissed her. In his exuberance, he almost missed
her lips completely, most of the kiss ending up on the side
of her nose instead, but she giggled and, holding his face
between her hands, kissed him back full on the lips.*

*They lay back on the straw which Lazar had placed
against the wall to be used later on the floor of the coop,
and Lazar began to feel braver and less awkward. This
wasn't much different from when he and his cousin Gail
had explored each other behind the bedroom door, except
of course Chanka was much older than Gail had been
which made it more exciting. They lay there quietly, kissing and hugging, and all Lazar could think of was how to
maneuver his hand so that it would seem to accidentally
land on Chanka's small breast. While he was busy plotting
his next move, Chanka simply took his left hand and
placed it on her right breast, moaning softly when he
squeezed it, and when she did that her mouth opened and
her tongue somehow found its way into Lazar's mouth.*

*Lazar felt his penis getting hard between his legs and he
didn't know what to do because it seemed to be trapped inside his pants, strangely bent in half, and the harder it got
the more it hurt. He wanted to pull his pants away a little
so it could straighten out, but he didn't know how to do
that without calling it to Chanka's attention and that
would be embarrassing. Besides, she was lying on his right
arm, now numb from the weight of her body, and to use*

his left hand would mean letting go of her breast, which he had not stopped fondling since she had first placed his hand there.

It was a terrible predicament and getting rapidly worse, but again Chanka came to the rescue. Rolling toward him onto her left side and pressing her right thigh between his legs, she managed both to unbend his erection, which now throbbed excitingly between his stomach and her bare thigh, and to remove most of the weight from his right arm which allowed him to reach around with that hand to her right breast as he shifted his left hand to her left breast. Clearly the more sexually aggressive of the two, in spite of Lazar's having made the first move (although thinking about it afterward, he was never altogether certain about that), Chanka giggled again, shifting slightly so that Lazar's penis was now pressed between her legs instead of against her thigh, and this time her tongue sliding into Lazar's mouth was no accident. It was Lazar's turn to moan.

During all of this, the pigeons had begun to return and there was now such a racket of cooing and fluttering about that finally, too distracted to continue, Chanka murmured that it was time for her to go home. The two got up, brushed the straw from their clothes, and went back down the ladder. Standing next to the house, they then exchanged their first words since going up to the loft an hour before.

"I'll come again to see your pigeons sometime."

"I would be happy to show them to you again."

They shook hands. Chanka turned and skipped away through the gate and down the street. Lazar went into the house.

. . . This was my first experience with a girl. I must say I really liked it. I told Frumke about it and she had a good

laugh, but she told me not to do that again. I kept no se-
crets from my sister, she was the only one I had to confide
in. I was lucky that my father was asleep at the time. However, I quickly forgot about it as I had work to do.

5. ↯

Uncle Moshe was my father's twin brother. He lived a few
blocks away from us with Aunt Esther and Cousin Mincha
in a small wood frame house with a stable connected to it.
Behind the stable was a swampy area leading to the river.
The house was very small and inside it was very plain. My
aunt and uncle were both very stingy.

In the winter Aunt Esther sold apples and pears in the
market. She had a yearly stall there and no matter how
cold it got she was always at that stall with the fruit spread
out on a platform that was covered with blankets and with
a clay pot filled with coals under her dress to keep her
warm. If I would pass her stand and ask her for an apple,
she always gave me the worst one she could find. But if my
cousin Mincha was there instead, she would pick out a
good one for me.

Uncle Moshe was very different from my father, rougher
and tougher, and he had no desire to learn the Talmud. He
also drank heavily. In addition to Mincha, there were three
sons and another daughter, Rachel, who were all in America. One day Rachel disappeared from the streets of New
York City and no one ever heard of her again. When my
uncle found out, he started to drink even more and my father couldn't do anything with him about his drinking.

During the winter, while Aunt Esther sold their fruit
from the summer before, Uncle Moshe worked as a cabby.
His carriage was of very poor quality. While the other cab-
bies had light carriages with rubber wheels and took good

care of their horses, Uncle Moshe's carriage had heavy iron wheels and it was very hard for his horse to pull. When my uncle would have too much vodka, the poor horse got nothing to eat. My aunt would just let him run loose in the swamp to find food for himself. I don't know how that horse survived all those years.

One day Uncle Moshe was driving his carriage to the cab stand near the railroad station and he fell from his seat into the hind legs of his horse . . .

Lazar was walking down the street, just passing the hotel when he noticed a crowd of people standing around a carriage which seemed to be stopped in the middle of the street. Two policemen were pushing their way through the crowd. It looked as though there might have been an accident and Lazar decided to investigate. He changed direction, crossed the street, and started walking toward the crowd.

All of a sudden he recognized the carriage. It was Uncle Moshe's! Lazar started running and reached the carriage just as the policemen were dragging his uncle from beneath the carriage. His uncle's eyes were closed and his face was bleeding and discolored. His glasses were still on but broken and the metal frame was bent all out of shape. Lazar was frightened. He suddenly felt sick to his stomach and started to cry.

"Uncle Moshe! Uncle Moshe! Are you all right?"

"Is this your uncle, boy?" asked one of the policemen.

"Yes," said Lazar, wiping his eyes with the heel of his hand. "What's the matter with him, is he dead?"

"No, he is unconscious and he doesn't look too good, but he smells like he's drunk too, so it's pretty hard to tell," said the policeman. "We'll put him in the carriage and help you drive him home."

The policemen eased Uncle Moshe down on the seat of

the carriage and sat down facing him. Lazar got up on the driver's seat, took the reins, and drove to his uncle's house. He was still shaken from the experience, but beginning to settle down with the responsibility of driving the carriage, and thinking ahead: We'll have to get the doctor ... How will we break the news to Father? ... I'll tell Mother first and she'll know what to do.

It wasn't that Lazar was close to Uncle Moshe. He didn't even like him. But Uncle Moshe was Father's twin brother and that made him somehow special, as though he was actually a part of Father, and all Lazar could think about was how his father would take it if anything really bad happened to Uncle Moshe. When Lazar started to pray to God not to let anything happen to Uncle Moshe, he was really praying for his father.

... We put him to bed and sent for Dr. Weiner. The doctor came and examined Uncle Moshe, but he said there was nothing he could do and he didn't think Uncle Moshe would recover. He said it was a combination of too much heavy drinking and a weak heart, and it was only a matter of time.

We all went to synagogue to pray and Aunt Esther went to the Rabbi to buy Uncle Moshe a middle name, which was an Orthodox Jewish custom to try to give a person new life. But nothing seemed to help. Uncle Moshe was in a deep sleep and snoring loudly.

We kept the news from my father, who had been acting very strangely anyway. The afternoon my uncle fell out of his carriage, my father got sick and stayed in bed. He refused to eat anything, he just slept and snored. Whenever we would wake him up to eat something, he would get angry at being awakened. Then he would drink a little tea and fall asleep again. This had been going on for two days. On the third day my Uncle Moshe died.

Mother and I went to the funeral, Frumke stayed home with Father. We still didn't tell him about Uncle Moshe. The next day Father woke up feeling much better and he got out of bed, but then he started asking about Uncle Moshe, about why hadn't he been to the house in almost a week, and we had to make up excuses. Uncle Schmuel hadn't been over either, because he was sitting shiva for Uncle Moshe, and Father started to miss him too.

After eight days, Uncle Schmuel came over and we took him aside to tell him that Father still hadn't been told. Uncle Schmuel said that was the right thing to do. But after a month or two, Father suspected the truth. He said he knew that Uncle Moshe had died, but he wanted us to tell him what had happened. When we told him, he was very upset but he didn't cry. He sat shiva and then insisted that I take him to the cemetery. At the grave he prayed and talked to himself very quietly. I couldn't hear what he was saying, but it seemed to me that he was talking to his twin brother.

From that day on, Father started to go downhill. He didn't care for food and ate just enough to get by. He seemed very removed from everything and began to read and pray more than ever, although he did say that he thanked God that he had at least one brother left to come see him once in a while.

Chapter Three

1. ࢤ

In the winter of 1913 rumors spread that Russia and Germany might go to war. Nobody paid much attention to the rumors, but by the next spring a lot of new recruits came to our army post for training and it looked as if Russia was beginning to mobilize. When that happened, many of the young men of Volkovysk started to run away. Finally, there was a proclamation that anyone caught running away from the draft would be shot, and that put an end to that. My parents were thankful that my brothers were all in America and that I was too young to be drafted.

In August, fighting broke out about six hundred kilometers from Volkovysk on the Austrian-Polish border near Krakow. That part of Poland was under the Russian flag. We started to feel the effect of war very quickly, because our stores couldn't get merchandise. All of the trains were busy with the military, carrying soldiers and equipment, and unless you were connected with army work you couldn't even take a train from our station.

There was no newspaper in Volkovysk, so the only news we had about the war was from people passing through town. Russia wasn't doing very well. The Germans were well inside of Russian territory and had taken thousands of prisoners. We knew the Germans had better generals, but thought that our army was so much bigger that it would win.

One day I was at the train station watching new recruits arrive for their six weeks of training while another batch was being shipped off to the Front, and an officer dropped a newspaper on the ground. I picked it up. It was from Moscow. Since I knew how to read Russian, I brought the paper home and read it to my parents. One article said the Germans had penetrated deeper into our lines and our troops had to retreat. However, they burned most of the towns behind them and blew up the bridges, so that nothing was left for the Germans.

The article went on to say that although it was necessary to withdraw, our troops had inflicted a lot of damage to the enemy, wounding and killing them by the thousands. Nothing was mentioned about our own losses. It ended by saying that Russia would never lose this war, regardless of how far it was necessary to retreat, and that Russia would destroy the enemy no matter how long it would take to do it.

On another page there was an article about how the Russian Government was telling the people of Poland, especially loyal Russians, that they should leave their homes with all of their belongings and livestock and travel far into Russia, because otherwise the Germans would take everything from them and make them slaves . . .

At the north end of town was the main highway running from Warsaw to Moscow. Lazar had heard that there were many refugees traveling on the highway and had decided to take a look for himself, but he certainly wasn't prepared for what he now saw. Stretched out before him, as far as he could see to the southwest in the direction of

Warsaw and to the northeast toward Minsk and Moscow, the highway was clogged with wagons and carriages of every description, loaded with household goods, chairs and tables and beds, farm tools, chickens and ducks and geese in wooden cages, merchant wagons with barrels of flour and salt, or dry goods, cows, goats, horses, dogs, even pigs, trailing behind the wagons, and everywhere there were people walking alongside the wagons because there was no room left inside, old people bent from long years in the fields, children darting in and out from between the wagons, laughing and having fun as if the whole thing were a long vacation just for them, mothers carrying babies in kerchiefs around their necks, men leading the horses, it was more people than Lazar had ever seen!

For a while he simply stood there and watched, overwhelmed by the magnitude of the scene before him. Only a few days ago you could have stood on this very spot for a whole morning and not counted more than half a dozen wagons moving on the highway in both directions. Now there were hundreds and hundreds of them, maybe thousands, all going in only one direction . . . east, away from the fighting and the Germans.

And the noise! Lazar had never in his life heard so much noise! He tried putting his fingers in his ears to shut it out, but it was no use. It was as if all of the people and all of the animals and even the creaking, rumbling wagons were clamoring for attention at once. But soon the strangeness of the scene became less frightening, and as Lazar watched, a kind of order began to emerge from what had at first appeared to be complete chaos.

Everything was moving very slowly, almost dreamlike in its slowness. People had long since given up trying to make time. There was no way to go around it and no way to speed up or get ahead of this slowly moving and seemingly endless stream of people, animals and wagons. There was also no way to sustain that sense of urgency with which they had fled from their homes in the first place, and so panic had finally given way to a quiet fatalism. If the Germans caught up, they caught up. There was no sense in worrying about it. All one could do now was keep moving or pull over to the side for a rest. There was no way to go back.

Nobody was on the same time schedule. Routines of a lifetime had been turned upside down. There was no plan. No morning, no afternoon, no evening. There was just keep moving. When people wanted to sleep or to cook a hot meal or repair a broken wheel, they pulled their wagon to the side of the road and stopped for a while. The stream continued to move, day and night, at the same slow pace of perhaps a few kilometers per hour. If you were to stand slightly above the highway and look down, as Lazar now stood on the small hill at the north end of town, you would see three lines . . . two stationary and thin, one on each side of the highway; and one wide line moving slowly and steadily between them.

His curiosity finally overcoming his shyness, Lazar walked among the wagons stopped at the side of the road.

"Hey, boy, what town is this?"

"Volkovysk."

"Do you know anyone who would like to buy a cow or two pigs?"

"No, I'm sorry, I don't. Where are you from?"

"Zyrardow."

"Why did you leave your home?"

"Haven't you heard? The Germans are coming! And the Russians are burning everything as they retreat! There's probably nothing left of our town by now."

At the next wagon they tried to sell Lazar a chicken. He told them he had no money. Everywhere, people were trying to sell their livestock but were equally unsuccessful with others from Volkovysk, who by now were beginning to realize that they too might soon be in the same predicament.

As Lazar moved along the line of wagons, he spoke to people. The story was always the same. No one had actually seen or heard the fighting, but as it got closer to their towns refugees began to clog the roads and proclamations had been posted: leave or become slaves to the Germans. It was exactly the way the Moscow newspaper had described it.

"Where are you going?" Lazar asked at one wagon.

"Who knows? To Moscow!"

"Where will you stay when you get there?"

"Who knows? The Government told us to leave our homes, let the Government worry about where we'll stay. Maybe they'll have new homes for us when we get there. What difference does it make? There's nowhere else to go!"

A crowd was standing around one covered wagon, talking quietly among themselves. Now and then a woman appeared at the rear of the wagon and handed out a large pot which someone would fill with hot water from a larger pot hanging over a fire. Lazar asked what was happening. Someone smiled and said a baby was being born. Soon Lazar heard the sound of an infant crying inside the wagon. A cheer went up from the crowd. The woman with the pot stuck her head out the rear of the wagon, smiled and said: It's a boy! Again the crowd cheered its approval, everybody slapping the back of the young father who only moments ago had been chewing nervously on his pipe but was now beaming with pride.

A bottle of vodka was produced and handed to the new father. He tilted his head back with the bottle to his mouth and the crowd began to chant: One! Two! Three! . . .

Lazar continued down the line of wagons, the chanting of the crowd, now up to ten, suddenly ending with a loud cheer as the proud new father finally reached his limit of vodka. Lazar turned his head, smiling, perhaps to catch a glimpse of the new father being handed his son, and with his head turned he stumbled and nearly fell over the dead horse which now blocked his path, legs rigid and straight up in the air, eyes still open and staring at death. It was an old horse, old and thin, with every rib clearly defined and the stomach now swelling with gases.

Lazar walked around the dead horse, staring at it in horror. He looked around but no one else seemed to pay any attention to it. And now he noticed that there were other dead animals along the side of the road. He had been so busy with the people, he hadn't seen the dead animals. What had taken on the character of an almost festive parade, especially highlighted by the joy of the crowd with the newborn baby, now took on a more somber tone. For the first time, Lazar understood the tragedy and hardship of the refugees who had left their homes against their will and were now making this long journey to a faraway city that was only a name.

Once again he became frightened, this time by the thought that he and Frumke and Mother and Father might have to join these people and become refugees too, that the dead dog he now passed could easily be his Rosetka or that the dead cow he saw in the field over there could be Belka! Lazar stopped, took one more look at the people on the highway, turned and ran all the way home.

... The next day I walked to the market which was also crowded with refugees. They were buying whatever they could, but the merchants were getting low on stock. There was no way to reorder merchandise for shipment by rail because of the war. The only way to transport goods now was by horse and wagon. A merchant from Bialystok was looking for someone to drive his two horses and a wagon loaded with expensive silk to Slonim, which was about thirty hours to the east by horse and wagon. He couldn't get anyone, so I told him I would do it. He said I was too young but if he couldn't get anyone else, he would let me do it.

I went home and told my parents, and as usual they didn't approve. However, my uncle Schmuel was there at the time and he said he would go with me and split the ten rubles between us, five for him and five for me. Mother agreed. I went back to the merchant and told him my uncle would go with me and he gave me the job. The weather was nice and warm. We left at five P.M. on a Tuesday, figuring we would arrive in Slonim late Wednesday night, unload the next morning and be home before Sabbath.

What I didn't know was that one horse was blind, but he was the bigger and stronger of the two, so I put him in the *oglobi,* the two poles that come out of the wagon. I put the second horse alongside as a helper. That was a big mistake, but I didn't find that out until later. The road was pretty level and we rode along doing fine until it started to get dark. We started to go down a steep hill. The wagon was heavily loaded and the harness on the blind horse was poor. It didn't have straps to go around behind his body to keep the collar in place at the lower part of his neck. The result was that going downhill the collar was pushed up his neck to his head and there was no way for him to hold the wagon back. The reins were useless because he couldn't turn his head, and he couldn't see where to run because he was blind, but of course neither of us knew that yet. My uncle didn't know very much about anything.

The wagon was beginning to pick up speed and would soon be out of control. I jumped off and ran to get hold of his halter so that I could lead him to the center of the highway, but that didn't help very much. Thank God there was a big pile of road cinders on the side of the highway and somehow that horse ran up the pile and stopped on top with the wagon. I started to yell at the horse and then I realized that he was blind. I got smart and switched horses, putting the one that could see in the lead. My uncle was still sitting on top of the wagon. He was happy to just let me do the work.

We traveled until about midnight and then stopped to rest. I watered the horses and gave them some oats. The bag of oats was from a new crop and it's not good to give them too much. We lay down to sleep for a couple of hours and woke up at daybreak. I looked around and saw the seeing horse was lying on the ground. I thought he was resting, but when I got closer I heard him moaning and groaning and his belly was blown up like a balloon. I asked my uncle what it could be, but he didn't know. He said it looked like the horse was dying.

I looked around for the blind horse and saw he was grazing in the field. I asked Uncle Schmuel: Didn't you tie them to the wagon last night? and he said he thought he had but he might have forgotten. Then I noticed the bag of oats was open and half gone. I understood what had happened. The horse had eaten too much of the new oats, had gotten bound up and was now loaded with gas. I tried to get him up but he wouldn't budge.

Somehow I knew what to do. I reached into his rectum as far as I could and pulled out a handful of shit. I kept doing that until I got out as much as I could. Then I pressed his belly and he started to leave a lot of gas. He stopped moaning but I still couldn't get him up. There was nothing I could do but wait for help. In a little while, two wagons came along and I told the drivers what had happened. They said I had done exactly the right thing.

They helped me to get him on his feet. Uncle Schmuel and I took turns walking him around for about two hours. Then he started to drink a lot of water and eat grass, farting and dropping shit all over until his stomach was back to normal and we could continue our journey. We got near Slonim about four A.M. and stopped to rest and feed the horses. There were other wagons returning empty to Bialystok from Slonim. One of the Jewish *balagools* (drivers) told my uncle not to take me with him into Slonim because the police were rounding up all the youngsters for work. My uncle arranged with this man for him to take me with him and drop me in Volkovysk on his way to Bialystok.

I was happy to be going home. The wagon was empty and we made good time. The balagool's name was Berrol, a man of about fifty years with a red beard, about six feet tall and a hundred and sixty pounds. I had some black bread with me and he had some black bread and cheese. We stopped at an inn about halfway there and we got hot potato soup and tea. Mine cost fifteen kopecks, he paid more because he had meat with his soup.

We didn't stay too long because he wanted to get to Bialystok before Sabbath. We arrived at Volkovysk about three A.M. Friday morning and he let me off on the highway in back of the army post. It was a very dark night and I had about two miles to walk. I don't mind telling you I was scared. I walked as fast as I could and cried until I got to the city streets. Every dog along the way must have barked at me.

I woke up Frumke and she let me in. It was about four-thirty. My parents heard us and they got up. They were happy to see me, but when I told them the whole story my mother started to cry and my father said he told her not to let me go. I said why get upset now, I'm home. Besides, I was hungry. Frumke made me eggs and tea with bread and cheese and by time I finished eating, it was daybreak. Father got dressed and started to pray, thanking God for my safe return.

Uncle Schmuel arrived about six P.M. just in time for Sabbath. He came to our house the next day after sundown and gave my mother the five rubles. He too had come back with a balagool in an empty wagon, but he was lucky, he didn't have to walk home in the dark from the highway. Father told his brother that he should have been awake when I was sleeping and the whole thing with the horse eating the new oats wouldn't have happened.

We all had fresh tea and sponge cake that Mother made to celebrate my safe return. So after all was said and done, I was happy. I was home safe and sound, I had done the trip almost all by myself anyway, and I had earned five rubles.

2. ל

There was very little money coming into the house. The summer had been very dry so far, the farmers said it was the worst dry spell in twenty years, and most of our early vegetables didn't come up. We prayed for rain.

On Sunday I walked to the market. Our town had changed a great deal. No more Sunday parades, no more high brass sitting outside the hotel. Only wagons of refugees passing through. The farmers' stalls were practically empty and the merchants were almost out of goods. The Germans continued their advance and were now near Warsaw. At this rate, they would be fighting near us in two or three months.

I passed by City Hall on the way home and there was a proclamation nailed to the door telling all loyal citizens to pack up and leave because the army would burn everything to the ground so there would be nothing left for the Germans. I was really frightened. What if a fire broke out around us? Where could we run? And with what?

When I got home I told Mother about the proclamation and suggested that we buy a horse and wagon, so that if we had to leave there would be room for us, for Uncle Schmuel and his wife and daughter, and for Aunt Esther and Cousin Mincha. The answer was no, that we couldn't afford to feed another animal, that if we didn't have to go we would be stuck with a horse we didn't need, and that if they burned the fields there would be no feed anyway.

I said that we had enough room in our barn to store feed while it was still available. The answer was still no. I didn't like it. I told Mother: You're a woman, what do you know of such things? It was the first time I ever said anything like that to my mother and I was very sorry afterward.

The whole month of July we didn't get a drop of rain. Our garden was ruined. If we didn't get rain soon, there would be nothing for the army to burn in the fields, they would already be burned. One day I walked into the jewelry store to see Joe. He was glad to see me, but angry that I had not been around to see him for so long. I promised that I would spend a weekend with him on the farm soon.

My old boss, Mazer Charkoff, asked me if I would like to come back to work for him. I told him that I would love to but I was needed at home. I asked him what he would do if the city would be on fire. He said he wasn't going anywhere, come what may, and that you couldn't believe everything that you heard these days. He thought I had a good idea about getting a horse and wagon in case of emergency, especially because of Father, but he told me not to listen to all the rumors. Still, once I got the idea in my head, I couldn't get rid of it.

By the first week of August we finally got two days of rain, but it was too late to help our garden. The Germans had now taken Warsaw and many of the villagers nearby were beginning to pack their belongings. Mother and Aunt Esther walked to one of the villages to see what they could buy, but the villagers had already sold what they managed to salvage of their crops. However, they did have a lot of potatoes and they said help yourself and take as much as you want. The question was how to get the potatoes home once we dug them out?

I was with Mother and Aunt Esther at the time and I suggested that we buy some kind of cheap horse and

wagon, which we could then sell after we got enough potatoes home for the three families. They agreed. As we were
walking home I saw an old peasant with a little horse and
wagon. I stopped him and asked if he knew of someone
who wanted to sell a horse and wagon cheap, and he said
he would sell us that one, horse, wagon, harness and all, for
twenty rubles. We told him we only had fifteen rubles with
us and he agreed. We paid him and drove home.

We were about eight kilometers from home. The horse
wouldn't run, only walk, and every once in a while he
would stop to rest. When I got him into the barn I fed him,
but he ate very little. I told our neighbor about our bargain
and when he looked at the horse, he said the horse was
more than twenty years old and if I fed him boiled potatoes and cooked oats he might just be able to drag the
wagon with a few sacks of potatoes in it. I didn't tell that to
my mother and Aunt Esther, I just prayed he would live
long enough to get the potatoes home.

The following Sunday, Mother, Frumke, Aunt Esther,
Mincha and I started out with the horse and wagon. Naturally, we all walked alongside the wagon so the horse
wouldn't get too tired. I was only afraid we would have to
put the horse in the wagon and pull him. At the end of the
day we had ten sacks of potatoes which we loaded onto the
wagon. The poor horse was pulling very slowly and stopping whenever he felt like it to rest, which was pretty often, but at every hill he just stopped altogether and refused to move no matter what we did. So we had to unload,
carry the sacks to the top of the hill and load again.

This went on for ten days, until finally we had enough
potatoes to last all of us for the winter. Then I put the word
out that I had a horse and wagon for sale very cheap. The
next day a poor man came who was crippled. I told him
that the horse was very old, which he said he could see for
himself, and I told him about having to cook his food too,
but he said that was all right. I sold him everything for six

rubles. The wagon was worth more than that alone, so he was happy. A few days later I heard that the horse died. I felt sorry for the poor man, but I had told him everything I knew about the horse, including that he couldn't pull a big load, so my conscience was clear.

3. ᚅ

The war was going badly and the fighting was getting closer. Rumors continued to spread that it wouldn't be long before the fighting reached Volkovysk. I started talking again to my parents about a horse and wagon and after many arguments and a lot of crying, I finally got them to say yes.

Thursday of that week I went to the market. There were several horses for sale, but I was looking for a complete outfit and there was none. The following Monday I went again and this time, as luck would have it, a Jewish merchant from Bialystok had sold his load of merchandise and was now selling his whole outfit. I ran all the way home and told Mother about it, and she went to our cousin who knew about horses. He came with us to bargain for it.

The merchant was anxious to sell and get home, so we bought it cheap for seventy-five rubles. The horse was a big black gelding about eight years old and sixteen hands high, and the wagon was a strong one with a good harness for the horse. I drove him home and I was so excited that I couldn't eat or sleep that night. The first thing I did was to tell Joe and he came to see my horse. He was amazed we got him so cheap. He told me I could come any weekend with my horse and graze him with the other horses.

I fixed a bigger stall for him in the barn, because the old stall I had made for the other horse was too small for this one. Belka seemed to enjoy the company of another animal. Then I started looking for ways to use the horse and wagon in order to earn back the money they had cost us. I arranged to do some hauling for the butcher and the baker. For the butcher I went to the slaughterhouse twice a week and for the baker I went to the mill once a week. It wasn't much but it was a start and it helped pay for the feed. In the meantime I felt a lot safer knowing we had a way to leave if we had to.

One Friday afternoon I waited for Joe to get out of work and told him that I could spend the weekend with him if that was all right. He was glad. He told me to get my horse and come out, so I rode out on horseback to their farm . . .

After the noon meal, Lazar and Joe walked to the big tree in the meadow behind the farmhouse, Joe picking his way slowly on his crutches, Lazar leading his horse at the end of a long rope because he was still a little afraid the horse might run away. It was a warm sunny day and they both felt lazy and relaxed after the big Sabbath meal. They sprawled out in the shade under the tree, Lazar's horse securely tied to a fence post and grazing contentedly on grass and clover. They watched in silence as his tail swished from side to side keeping the flies away. Finally, Joe broke the silence.

"I hate my job. I'm working on these goddamn little pocket watches now and it's hard on my eyes. I'm gonna go blind."

"Why don't you find another job?"

"What the hell else can a cripple like me do but sit on a bench? I hate to say it but it looks like I'm going to work on damned pocket watches the rest of my life. Oh the hell with it, who cares? Let's talk about girls. How's your love life?"

Lazar told him all about Chanka and about their pet-
ting session in the loft next to the pigeon coop.
"Yeah, but did you fuck her?"
"Who, me? I wouldn't do anything like that, I'm not
even twelve yet! And she's only a year older than me. I
don't even know how to do it. Besides, I think you should
wait until you're married and I have a long time before I'll
be old enough to get married."
Joe laughed. "Lazar, that's old-fashioned. People don't
think that way anymore."
"What about you?"
Joe shrugged. "Who'd want a cripple like me? I have a
hard time even getting around on crutches. I don't social-
ize. I don't go out with anybody. You're about the only
friend I have. I just sit on a bench and fix pocket watches."
He sounded so bitter that Lazar didn't know what to say
to that. Again there was a long silence as they stared at the
horse. Joe was frowning, as if he were thinking about
something serious. Suddenly he looked at Lazar and said,
"Can you keep a secret?"
"Sure. What?"
"I'm in love."
"You're what? Who with?"
"Swear you won't tell? I don't dare let anybody know."
"I swear! Who is it?"
"It's a girl on our farm, the daughter of one of the Rus-
sian farmhands. She's fifteen going on sixteen, her name is
Katanya and she's very pretty. She always helps me har-
ness my pony in the morning and loads the milk cans onto
the wagon that I deliver in the city on my way to work. I
don't know how it happened, it just happened.
"One Sabbath morning, my parents went into town for
services at the synagogue and I was home alone. Katanya
came over to ask if I needed anything and I said the only
thing I need is a girl like you to love. I was only kidding
around, you know, but she laughed and said, 'Well I'm a

*girl, you can love me.' I said oh sure, a cripple like me. And
she told me as far as she was concerned only my leg was
crippled and the rest of me looked okay to her. Then she
sat down next to me on the couch and she kissed me.*

*"I figured hell, what have I got to lose? So I kissed her
for a while and I felt up her tits. Does she have nice tits!
Then I put my hand under her dress and she didn't seem to
mind that either. She had no pants on and her pussy was
all wet and creamy. Then she opened my pants and took
out my cock and started to play with it. By now we were
both hot as hell and I asked her if she had ever gone all the
way. She said there was one way for me to find out.*

*"So I got on top of her and it was hard getting it in, but I
did and it felt great, only I couldn't hold back and it was
over pretty quick. She was bleeding a little and started to
cry, and she said, 'Is that it? I expected so much more!' I
guess she didn't enjoy it very much. I admitted it was my
first time too and that's why I came so fast, but I told her
next time would be better because neither of us would be
scared. She didn't say very much after that, she just looked
at me funny and left."*

*Lazar had never heard talk like this before. It excited
him, he knew that. No one had ever told him what it was
like, nor even how it was done. Once, he had seen the
neighbor's dogs doing it but he couldn't get close enough
to watch. He had never been able to visualize how people
did it. Whenever he asked Frumke, she just said it wasn't
something to talk about. It occurred to him that Joe was
taking a big chance.*

*"You could get in a lot of trouble, Joe," he said. "Is it
worth the risk? What if she gets a baby? She's Russian and
you're a Jew. If her father finds out he might kill you! Or
he might try to make you marry her, and then your father
might kill you. Boy, you're really taking chances!"*

*"Listen, Lazar, when you get that hot you don't think
about things like that. I'd have fucked her if her old man*

*had been in the next room! She's the first girl that ever
looked at me twice and she doesn't care about my leg. I'm
eighteen and I've never had a woman before. I don't give a
damn what happens. Nobody cares a shit about me and all
I have to look forward to is a life of crutches and pocket
watches. Hell, if she lets me I'll fuck her every day and
twice on Sunday. She's beautiful. Wait till you meet her,
then you'll understand. If you want to wait until you get
married, that's your business. Me? I'll take it where I can
get it!"*

... At sundown I took my horse and rode home. I
couldn't stop thinking about Joe and wondering what
would come of his love affair with Katanya.

For the next couple of weeks I was busy bringing in what
vegetables were still left in the garden and with trying to
round up enough feed for the livestock, which wasn't so
easy because of the dry summer. Everything was getting
scarce and people were trying to stock up on what supplies
were still available, because most of the merchants were
beginning to run out.

The flow of refugees through our town had just about
stopped. Now the highway was full of soldiers heading for
the front lines. The fighting had reached Bialystok and the
rumors were that in a month at the most the fighting
would reach us. It was very frightening. We could already
hear the rumbling of distant artillery and see the flashing
of the big guns at night!

I managed to buy a load of hay at the market, but I still
couldn't locate any grain. I went to the jewelry store and
asked Joe if he knew where I could buy oats and chicken
feed. He said he would get off from work early on Friday
and I should meet him at the farm with my horse and wagon.
Then we would drive to his sister's about twenty kilometers
from the farm, spend Sabbath there, and on Sunday morn-

ing when the peasants brought their grain to his brother-in-law's mill, I would be able to buy what I needed . . .

As soon as they left the farm and started down the road, Joe began to tell Lazar the latest developments in his love affair with Katanya.

"Two days after that first time, she came to me and said she wanted to try it again, but I told her not until I got protection so she wouldn't get pregnant. She wanted to know what a rubber was. She didn't understand. I told her to meet me in the loft of the barn right after dark the next day. She got really angry with me and ran off."

"You mean you actually said no to her?"

"Well you're the one who started me thinking about getting her in trouble and what her father might do!"

"So then what, did she meet you in the loft?"

"Ha! She was waiting with bells on! By the time I got there she was so hot she lifted her skirt and said, 'Zachade! Get in and push!' This time I lasted a lot longer and just as I came, she did too and she said, 'Ya loblo tebya . . . Joe, I love you!' We lay in each other's arms for a while and then we did it again, and we've been doing it three or four times a week ever since. You know, Lazar, I really love her. What the hell am I going to do?"

"Joe, you're playing with fire! Why can't you just do it with her and not love her? That way you can both have a good time and then one day she'll find a Russian boy to marry her."

"I couldn't stand that, her marrying somebody else. I told you, I love her!" Joe was upset at the thought of Katanya being with somebody else. "What would you do, Lazar, if it was you?"

Of course Lazar had no experience to compare this to, he was so much younger than Joe, but he didn't think it strange that Joe would ask him for advice. After all,

they were friends. Lazar never thought about the age dif-
ference between them and neither did Joe.

"I would tell my sister everything and ask her advice.
Your sister is married, maybe she can help you, or your
brother-in-law. They know more than I do about such
things. It just seems to me it's pretty sudden. It's only been
a few weeks!"

"I'd marry her tomorrow if she'd agree. My father isn't
very religious, I don't think he would object. Mother is
more religious, though. I don't know what she would say.
As for Katanya's parents, I don't know what they would
say but they're very poor. With one sister married and my
other sister and brother in America, the farm will one day
belong to me. And they have three other kids to worry
about. I don't think they would mind too much. They've
been on the farm since I was born. They like me."

They were approaching Joe's sister's place. The sun was
almost down.

"My advice is to forget the whole thing," Lazar said as
he turned off the road and headed toward the farmhouse.
"You're too young to get married. Have a good time in the
hayloft and get marriage out of your mind."

"Maybe so, I don't know. I'll tell you, Lazar, I'm glad I
can at least talk to you about it. If I couldn't talk to some-
body about this, I'd go nuts. You're the only friend I have."

It made Lazar feel very mature to be off on his own for
the weekend, in his own horse and wagon, and have his
friend who was so much older than he was ask his advice
in a love affair.

"That's all right," Lazar answered, "that's what friends
are for." Joe was the only friend he had too.

4.

Volkovysk was becoming an armed camp. Soldiers were everywhere. Artillery was being placed on the mountains surrounding the city. Kitchens were set up in the market for the soldiers and you could smell cabbage and pork cooking. On the outskirts of town, soldiers were digging trenches in the fields. And at night the sound of the big guns was getting closer. It sounded like thunder.

The town itself was still peaceful and the soldiers were well behaved. The tearooms and whorehouses were doing a lot of business. But with all the artillery around, there were also a lot of horses, and the army began to buy up most of the hay and oats that were still available. I didn't have a lot of feed for my livestock and I was worried, but our neighbors started to hide their feed and they promised to help me when I needed it.

One day there was a proclamation that the army needed more horses and it was your loyal duty to sell your horse to the army if you had one. I took my horse into one of our empty apartments, put him in the kitchen and locked the door from the outside. The next week the local police came to us for our horse and we said we sold him. They looked around and couldn't find him, so they believed our story. I also took two wheels off the wagon and hid them.

In a few days the police stopped searching for horses, but I still kept my horse in the apartment. It was hard work, I had to keep a lot of straw under him so he wouldn't ruin the floor. At night I took him out and exercised him, then I put him in his stall while I cleaned out the manure from the kitchen and put down fresh straw.

When the weekends came, I would ride him out to Joe's farm on the back roads and stay there for two days while he ran in the fields and grazed. There was no danger because the army didn't bother the farmers about their horses.

It was very peaceful on the farm, away from the soldiers and the artillery, and you were never hungry in Joe's house because there was always a lot of good food to eat.

One night at Joe's, during Friday night prayers, Joe got up and went to his room. When everybody went to bed later, I asked him what was the matter. He said he had a hard day at his bench and the old man yelled at him because he broke a stem on one of the watches, but mostly he was worried because his father was beginning to suspect something was going on between him and Katanya.

His father had not asked him outright, but said he noticed that whenever Joe was home she was around more than when he wasn't home. Joe's father said that he didn't want any problems. I asked Joe if he was still doing it with Katanya and he grinned and said yes, three or four times a week and he was more in love with her than ever, but that whenever he told her he wanted to marry her, she just laughed and wouldn't give him a straight answer. I told him if I was him I would tell his father how he feels and if he didn't, there might be a lot of trouble.

The next morning there were Russian soldiers resting all over the fields and hundreds of artillery pieces drawn by horses. We talked to some of the soldiers. Most of them were very young. They said they were moving up to the Front and that Bialystok had been taken by the Germans. I didn't understand why the Germans were able to advance so fast. One of the Russian officers sat on the porch talking to Joe's father and he said the army wasn't worried about the Germans taking our cities. He said the plan was to retreat without too much fighting and draw the Germans deep into Russia until winter came and then to counterattack.

The soldiers rested for a few hours and then pulled out. After they left, Joe's father discovered they had cleaned out his barn. He now realized he'd better hide everything he could in the cellars and also to hire more men and harvest the fields. According to the Russian officer, the fighting would reach us in two weeks.

At sundown I left for home, feeling depressed about Joe and about the war and worried about where I was going to get enough feed for Belka and the horse. Since there was nothing left to buy in the market, I decided to try the villages. The next day Frumke and I drove about sixteen kilometers to a village where I was able to buy three bags of oats, one bag of chicken feed, one bag of wheat, and some hay and straw. One farmer told me I could have all the hay I wanted from his field for nothing, but I would have to rake it myself. Frumke and I returned with rakes and for the next three days we raked three wagonloads of hay which I then stored behind our brick building. I thanked the farmer and told him he was always welcome in our house for tea whenever he came to market.

Two weeks passed. The fighting was getting much closer. Trainloads of soldiers were arriving at the railroad station and marching to the army post. I followed them one day but was turned away at the gate. No one was allowed without a pass. On the way home I passed Chanka's and she was sitting on the porch. She was glad to see me. Her parents wouldn't let her come to my house because of all the soldiers in town. She asked if I still had my pigeons and I said no, I sold them because I was too busy with my horse now. Her mother and father came out of the store and we all talked for a while about the war. Then I left for home. Chanka walked part of the way with me. Then we kissed good-bye and I said I would try to come back again soon.

When I got home, Mother wanted to know where I was all day. She was upset and crying. Father had gotten ill and she had to send for the doctor. The doctor said it was his *shlepoya kishka* again and he gave my father some medication for his stomach, saying he would be back in a few days. I went in to see him but he was sleeping, so I went outside and helped Frumke bring in the last of the cabbages and beets from the garden.

It was almost dark when I finished and Father was up and feeling better. I sat with him and told him about my day, he always liked it when I would tell him about my daily activities. He wanted to know if I had been to synagogue for maariv, the evening prayers, and when I said I had been working in the garden and didn't have time, he got out the prayer book and we prayed together. Then he felt even better and came to sit with us at the table while we had dinner.

5. ‍

Thousands of soldiers and cavalry were going up and down the streets and no one knew what was going on. We heard that the Germans were now halfway between Bialystok and Volkovysk, but we couldn't figure out if the troops were going to the Front or if they were retreating. There was nothing but confusion. Even the soldiers looked confused and on edge, as if they didn't know where they were going either, and they weren't in a very good mood to talk to. All they wanted to know is where they could get girls.

Grocery stores were practically empty because the soldiers were cleaning them out. Sometimes they paid, sometimes they just took what they wanted and walked out. There was nothing the merchants could do about it. When they complained to the local police, the answer was oh well, that's war, be glad you're not in their shoes. Except for that, the soldiers were orderly and respected the local police.

We had about thirty men at our police station, plus ten mounted police for the rural areas. They were all in their forties, tall and well built, and almost all of them had handlebar mustaches and no beards. They wore wide gray pants that were draped over their boots, a loose shirt with a high neck and long sleeves, worn outside the pants and gathered at the waist with a wide belt. On the left side they wore a sword and on the right side a pistol. They wore a cap with a round top and a peak in front with a big emblem of the Tsar's face. In the winter they wore a long coat almost to the ankles with a *bashlick*, like a hood to put over their head when it was very cold and snowing.

One of the policemen was friendly with my family and used to stop at the house sometimes for tea and cake. I was afraid to drive alone for the butcher and baker, so I asked him if he would ride with me. He agreed to do so when he was off duty and that enabled me to continue to make the runs that week. The butcher gave him some meat for helping me and the baker gave him bread and rolls, so he was happy. We decided to wait to see how things were the next week before we decided to do it again.

By this time there was nothing left to buy in town but bread and meat, but Mother baked her own bread and Belka kept us supplied with milk and cheese, so we had plenty to eat and even had enough to share with our neighbors. Father was feeling better and as usual when he was feeling good, he studied the Torah and the Gemara, but he had nobody to debate with, so often he talked out loud. Sometimes Uncle Schmuel came, but my father always kept him debating for hours and he didn't like it, so he only came once in a while.

Uncle Schmuel's main income came from working as a traveling cantor for the small synagogues that couldn't afford a steady cantor, but now that traveling was impossible he wasn't working. You weren't permitted on the trains anymore and you didn't dare travel by horse and wagon because the soldiers would confiscate them. By now the city was at a standstill. Nothing was moving except for the military, which was everywhere. Infantry, artillery, cavalry, cherkesans and cossacks, plus wagons and supplies, all moving up and down our streets and roads.

On Friday I decided to take a chance and I rode my horse out to Joe's farm for the weekend. After prayers and dinner, we sat on the porch and talked about how long it would be before the Germans took over and what it would be like then. It was almost the end of September and in town the word was that it was now just a question of days.

As we talked Joe was very quiet and he looked really worried about something. Finally he got up and went inside. His father commented that Joe had "that damn girl on his mind" and I knew that Joe must have followed my advice and told his father about Katanya. His father said that he told Joe that he would never allow such a marriage and that he only hoped her father wouldn't find out because there was no telling what he might do.

The next morning Joe's parents walked to the small synagogue on the outskirts of town, about two kilometers from their house. It was a small synagogue and a very nice one, about halfway between Joe's house and mine. There were about a hundred or so in the congregation. It had nice wooden benches and the *aron kodesh* and the *bimah* were of beautifully rubbed mahogany. The *parokhet* was of heavy gold material and inside were four Torahs. As you entered the synagogue, there was a large oven on the left and the front of it was white tile. In front of that there was a bench and table where the older men studied the *khumesh* on Saturday afternoons. I had been to that synagogue many times because I liked the cantor there better than the one at our synagogue.

With Joe's parents gone, Joe came out of his room and sat with me on the porch. He explained that he had a big argument with his parents over his wanting to marry Katanya, and that his father had told him never to even mention her name again and to just pray her father never finds out. I asked Joe what he said then to his father and he said he told his father he didn't care what happens to him.

Just then Katanya came looking for Joe to tell him the good news that she just got a job as a kitchen helper on the ranch where her brother worked. Joe didn't want her to take the job because he didn't want her to leave the farm. He took her inside to his room and asked me to stay on the porch or take a walk. I knew what he wanted to do. I went to see how my horse was doing and I must have stayed there for quite a while, because then I saw Joe's parents walking back from synagogue. I ran to the house to warn Joe, but Katanya was already gone and Joe was in his room, undressed and crying. There wasn't time for him to tell me what happened, he just got dressed in a hurry, washed his face, and went out on the porch with me just as his parents reached the house.

At the noon meal Joe wasn't himself at the table. His parents could see something was wrong, but they didn't mention it. Afterward, they went to lie down in their bedroom and we went outside and Joe told me what happened with Katanya. He said he pleaded with her not to take the job, to marry him instead. She told him she couldn't because her father would never allow it and she was underage, so there was no point in talking about it, she was taking the job because her family needed the money. Then she told Joe she didn't want to waste time talking about marriage, she would rather talk about love. She lifted up her dress and she had nothing on underneath and she said, "Joe, I want you to *yab* me before I go away."

Joe said at first he didn't want to because he was so upset, but he couldn't resist her and it was the best time they ever had. Then she kissed him good-bye and said she would see him when she came to visit her family on holidays. I told Joe it was all for the best and that he was just lucky her father never found out. I felt that the reason Joe was so upset was he had got used to having it whenever he wanted it and now he didn't know what he was going to do for a woman, especially one who wouldn't mind that he was crippled. He admitted that was true. I told him not to worry, there were plenty of bardaks in Volkovysk.

That evening we all went out on the porch after dinner. We sat and talked for quite a while. I had the feeling that this would be my last weekend on the farm for a long time and it made me sad. It was almost dark and there was a chill in the air. Winter would arrive soon. We were just about to go inside when suddenly the whole sky turned red around the city. We also heard explosions. I was worried that the city was on fire the way some people had said it would be, that the Russians were burning everything down.

I said good-bye, ran for my horse, and galloped home as fast as my horse could carry me. When I got there my parents were worried and upset. I suggested we get everything ready to leave, but Father said we were not going anywhere, come what may. I went to the barn and got the wagon ready anyway. Then I walked over to the main street to see what was happening. It looked like the army post was burning, but the fire department didn't seem to be doing anything about it, so the Russians must have set it on fire themselves.

The street was full of soldiers. I didn't see anybody from town. The stores were all shut tight and some of the windows were boarded over. It was strange to see the town all lit up from the fire and the streets full of soldiers running around and shouting to each other. I got scared and ran back to the house. Later that night, Saturday 26 September 1914, the battle for our city began . . .

Lazar was asleep when the sound of the first barrage roared through the house. He had become accustomed to the sound of distant artillery the past few weeks, but this sounded like it was right on top of them and he was suddenly wide awake. The noise was deafening! Cabinet doors popped open and dishes smashed to the floor, the windows rattled as though they were about to break, Rosetka and the puppy stood barking at the front door as though the noise were an intruder trying to break in. Everybody was up and shouting at once.

"Mother!"

"Frumke! What is it? What's happening?"

"I don't know, Lazar! Mother! Father!"

The door to the bedroom burst open and Lazar's mother rushed out, shouting above the noise, "Lazar! Frumke! Get dressed! Hurry!"

"Golde! Where are my slippers? Where are my books? Come back here and help me get my books!"

The night sky was filled with splashes of orange and red, and the inside of the house took on an eerie quality in the flashing light. Lazar saw that his mother was already completely dressed. She must have slept in her clothes, he thought. His teeth had begun to chatter, partly from the shock of being awakened so abruptly from a sound sleep, partly from the cold because there was no fire. They had been warned against fires for the last two days. The smoke from the chimney would provide the Germans with an artillery target, they had been told, so fires were illegal.

Another barrage went off, shaking the house again, and now they could hear shells screaming overhead.

"Oh, Mother, what shall we do!" Frumke cried.

"Be calm! We are going next door to the brick house where it will be safer. Here, take the bread and cheese. Lazar, you carry the milk, be careful, don't spill it. Dovid, are you ready?" Their mother always took over in an emergency.

Dressed and loaded down with food and blankets, she led them quickly across the yard, Lazar's father moving slowly in the rear and carrying four of his precious books

*cradled in both arms, the dogs racing ahead and still bark-
ing nervously although the artillery barrages seemed to
have abated for the moment. They could hear machine-
gun fire in the distance. It was coming from somewhere
west of town.*

*Entering the brick house first, Lazar's mother banged on
a tenant's door, explaining to them when it opened that
they had come because the brick house would be safer. Another barrage of artillery exploded in the night and everyone rushed inside for cover. Tables and beds had been
pushed against the inside wall, away from the windows
for safety, and now they all huddled under the furniture,
all but Lazar's father who sat on the floor with his back to
the wall, bowed his head, and rocked gently in prayer.*

*Lazar was under a bed with the two dogs. For some rea-
son he was no longer afraid. The little children were crying and the women were doing their best to reassure them
that nothing would happen to them, but somehow Lazar
knew no harm would come to any of them. Rosetka shivered and he reached over to scratch behind her ears, mur-
muring, It's all right, Rosetka, shhh, it's going to be all
right now.*

*Then he remembered Belka and his horse. They must be
frightened too! No one noticed as Lazar crawled to the
door, reached up to the latch and opened it, crawled out
and closed the door behind him. Then he stood up, opened
the front door and went out into the yard. The guns were
no longer firing together in barrages but seemed to be
firing individually now, and Lazar paused for a moment,
trying to understand the nature of the battle.*

*The Russian guns were firing from the hills to the north
and northeast of town, their guns shelling the Germans in
the valley on the other side of Volkovysk, to the west of the
Russian trenches which Lazar had seen being dug the
week before. The German artillery, located in the valley,
was returning the fire and their shells were exploding up*

in the hills. For some reason nothing seemed to be happening to the city.

As the guns continued to fire, Lazar looked up and occasionally he could see what appeared to him to be small tree trunks flying through the air, accompanied by a kind of high-pitched screaming noise as they passed overhead. The sky was now a fiery red and the explosions sounded very near. One sounded so close that Lazar was startled and ran for the barn. Belka was making an awful racket and the horse was rearing in his stall and pawing the air, his nostrils flared, his eyes wide with fear.

Gradually Lazar calmed them down, stroking first one neck and then the other, speaking gently and soothingly as though they were little children and he was their father. Then he brought them water and hay and stayed with them until they were sufficiently calmed for him to return to the house, just as the sun was coming up.

"Lazar, my God, where have you been? We've been worried sick!"

"It's all right, Mother, I just went to the barn to take care of the animals. There was no need to worry, nothing is going to happen to us. All of the fighting is outside of the city, up in the hills and out in the valley. They are firing at each other over the top of us. Nothing is falling on the city. I saw it!"

"Lazar, don't go out again unless you ask your mother's permission, is that understood?"

"Yes, Father."

For the next two days and nights, the firing continued sporadically but without letup. There was no way of knowing which way the battle went. Everyone stayed in the house, except for occasional trips to the outhouse or the barn. There was no cooking because of an edict concerning fires, but there was plenty of bread, fruit, cheese and milk. Each morning and afternoon, Lazar's mother went to milk Belka, but the cow had other ideas. The artillery had made her skittish and now she either withheld her milk or ended up kicking the pail over in her excitement. The noise was simply too much for Belka's system. No one blamed her. It was beginning to be too much for everyone else's.

Tuesday morning, just after daybreak, the firing stopped. One notices noise immediately, but the absence of noise is more subtle and so no one realized it was gone until they heard birds chirping. It was a sound they had not heard in three days. Lazar opened the front door and peered out. Nothing seemed to be stirring in the street, so he closed it again. His father continued to pray.

About ten o'clock there was suddenly a commotion in the street. Lazar went to investigate. People were all emerging from their houses, smiling and waving to each other. Then a cheer went up and Lazar could see soldiers marching down the center of the street. It was the Germans. People were simply so relieved that the battle was over, that they were still alive and the city still intact, they didn't seem to care whether it was the Germans or the Russians who had won. Shopkeepers were opening their shops, the police were out attempting to keep order, and everyone was showing the Germans they weren't afraid. Even Lazar cheered, but he wasn't sure why.

Chapter Four

1. ৵

I was short on feed. I decided to harness my horse and drive to the mill for the two bags of grain I had left there to be ground. That was a big mistake. When I got to the mill and asked the owner for my feed, I learned that the Russians had taken everything before the Germans arrived and there was nothing that he could do about it. Now I was really worried about what I was going to do for feed.

I started back home, but about a block from my house a German soldier with a rifle slung across his back yelled at me: *Halt, junger Mann!* and he motioned for me to pull over to the side of the street. *Warten Sie hier,* he told me, wait here. Then I saw our local police directing other wagons to stop near me. Several more wagons driven by soldiers also lined up. Soon, wagons were being directed from other streets and a whole convoy was being lined up on the main street near the church. No one knew what for.

I asked one of the soldiers in Yiddish if I could run over to my house and tell my parents, and he said: *Ja, mach schnell!* I ran home and told Mother not to worry, that I wouldn't be alone because there were a lot of other wagons being gathered. I grabbed a piece of bread and a bag of hay and ran back. It was getting late in the afternoon and there must have been a hundred wagons by now. I asked the German soldier what we were going to do and he said: *Wir werden alle verwundeten Soldaten vom Schlachtfeld bringen*, which meant we were going to bring all the wounded soldiers from the battlefield . . .

It was nearly four in the afternoon by time the convoy of wagons was complete and ready to leave Volkovysk. Frumke stood by Lazar's wagon, crying.

"Oh, Lazar, I told you not to take your horse out today! Why didn't you listen to me?"

"Stop crying, nothing's going to happen to me. The soldier told me we're just going out to pick up the wounded and we'll probably be back tonight. I'll be all right. Go home now, Frumke, everybody's looking at me."

It was embarrassing to have his sister crying and bawling him out in front of all the other wagons. After all, there was nothing to worry about. It wasn't as though they were going to the Front, which had been the rumor earlier in the afternoon. Besides, he knew a lot of the other wagon drivers. About ten of them were Jewish, the rest were Russians and Poles and a few of them were from his own neighborhood. There were also ten German soldiers and two medics. As usual, Lazar was the only boy among the men.

They traveled for almost three hours along the road to Bialystok, until they reached a makeshift aid station where a large group of Russian and German wounded was gathered and waiting. The fading twilight glowed with a dozen small fires around which those wounded who could huddled together to keep warm, while the less fortunate lay shivering on stretchers nearby.

All afternoon, first as he waited with the other wagons in town and then driving in the convoy, Lazar had been excited, proud even, that he was the only boy there. It made him feel so much older, a man really, doing important things like men do and being treated like a grown-up by the other men. If only Chanka could see him now! And Mother and Father. Well, Mother would be worried, naturally, but then Mother was a woman, so what could you expect; but Father would understand that Lazar was a man now, doing a man's work, and could take care of himself.

At the aid station, Lazar's mood began to change. All around him men were moaning and sobbing in pain, and once, when he heard a voice cry out: Mutter! *he realized that even a grown man could cry for his mother. It was a frightening place to be in, even for a boy who was a man.*

One by one the wagons were loaded with wounded soldiers, and as Lazar waited his turn, he stared out at the open fields which only last month had probably been stacked with huge mounds of hay during the harvest, just like the fields at home, only now they were piled with mounds of broken artillery wagons, howitzers, machine guns, rifles and bayonets, and they were pockmarked with gaping holes from exploding artillery shells. Everywhere, as far as he could see, were the bodies of men and horses, twisted grotesquely in the violent death of battle. Lazar no longer felt proud and excited. He felt suddenly cold and empty and wished he was home.

"Boy! Get your wagon up here!" Lazar shivered, drew the blanket he had wrapped himself with closer around his shoulders and moved his wagon forward to the group of remaining wounded. He watched as five wounded soldiers were helped onto his wagon, three Germans and two Russians. One of the Russians was unconscious, blood oozing from a stomach wound. The other four were able to sit up. None talked, they just stared straight ahead, eyes dazed, faces blank. Lazar felt very sad and very much alone.

73

❧

It was ten o'clock by time all the wounded had been placed in wagons and the convoy set out, headed for the nearest field hospital in Bialystok. After several hours the Lieutenant in charge decided the convoy should rest for the night. There was no food, only water from a nearby stream. Lazar shared his piece of bread with the four wounded soldiers in his wagon. The fifth soldier was still unconscious and was now shivering. The other Russian took off his coat and used it to cover his comrade.

The horses were unhitched so they could graze in the field. Most of the drivers and wounded slept. Some, like Lazar who was simply too upset by now to possibly sleep, built a bonfire and sat around it to keep warm. Several times during the night, German troops with wagons full of equipment passed the convoy heading east. At daybreak, the German Lieutenant announced that he had learned during the night that the field hospital was not in Bialystok after all. The convoy headed back in the direction from which they had come the night before.

When they reached the place where the aid station had been, the convoy stopped and the German soldiers gathered around their Lieutenant and studied the map. Lazar glanced back and noticed that the Russian with the stomach wound didn't seem to be moving or making any noise and that the bandage was now completely soaked in blood. Frightened, he yelled for a medic. One of the two medics came over, peeked under the bandage and muttered, "Got im Himmel, est gibt nichts womit ich ihm helfen kann!" and walked away shaking his head. There was nothing he could do for the dying Russian soldier.

It was now eleven o'clock in the morning. The Lieutenant decided that the field hospital must be located in another city a day's travel to the north toward Grodno, and the convoy started out again. About an hour later, the Rus-

sian in Lazar's wagon died. The Germans decided there was nothing to be done with the dead until the field hospital was reached. The convoy stopped once during the afternoon for rest at a small village where they hoped to find food, but they soon discovered that the retreating Russian Army had cleaned everything out so there would be nothing for the Germans.

By nightfall the Lieutenant again learned that he was heading in the wrong direction and that there was no field hospital to the north, not even in Grodno, so once again the convoy turned around and headed back. By now everyone was complaining. The drivers were tired and hungry. If the wounded did not soon reach a hospital, many more would die. It was obvious that the convoy was going in circles. As the drivers became more vocal in their complaints, the German soldiers began to yell. They were tired and hungry too. Somehow, the Lieutenant managed to keep order. The convoy rested for two hours and then drove on through most of the night, Lazar and the other drivers dozing off and on in their seats while the horses pulled steadily on.

In the morning the Lieutenant learned at last that the hospital had been set up in Volkovysk all along. After two nights and almost three days of traveling in circles with no food and very little sleep, the wagons finally headed back to where they started. Near two in the afternoon, as if they had somehow silently decided among themselves, all of the horses stopped and refused to go on without rest. The convoy was near a small village about twelve kilometers from Volkovysk.

The horses were turned loose to graze and several of the drivers walked into the village looking for food. Lazar spotted a peasant he knew, a man who had come to his house to chop wood, and he quickly told the man about how they had been driving the wounded soldiers around aimlessly for three days without food. The peasant took

75

Lazar home and gave him half a bushel of potatoes, all he had to spare, and Lazar thanked him gratefully and ran back to the wagons with the potatoes.

He built a fire and roasted the potatoes, then cut them in half and distributed the halves until there were none left, eating two whole potatoes in the process. It was his first meal since leaving home for the mill. About four they started out again, finally reaching Volkovysk by sundown. Sure enough, a field hospital had been set up on the army post.

After the wounded had been taken off the wagons, the drivers were told that they could go home if they wished but that the horses and wagons must remain until morning. The Germans passed out bread, jelly, coffee, and apples to the drivers, a small portion of oats and hay for the horses. Lazar ate. Then he fed and watered his horse. He wasn't sure what to do. He wanted very much to go home but he was reluctant to leave his horse at the army post. He decided to take a chance.

Later in the evening, as the camp quieted down, he unhitched his horse and started to walk with him, first around the post as though he were merely exercising his horse, then heading toward the rear of the post. Lazar knew every inch of the army post from when he had serviced the clocks in the barracks and also from delivering cigarettes. He knew all of the back alleys and shortcuts.

Tense and frightened, making what he believed to be his escape from the German guards, but trying to act nonchalant at the same time, Lazar walked his horse slowly out the rear of the post. Then, at the first alley, he climbed up on his horse and rode bareback through the back fields until he arrived at last at the gate to his house.

Not until he was inside, hugging and kissing his family, did Lazar admit to himself how frightened and homesick he had been these last three days, though of course he said nothing of this as he told a greatly relieved mother and fa-

*ther and sister of his bold adventure on the road with the
convoy of wagons and soldiers.*

2. ४

The Germans stationed soldiers in every house in Volkovysk, so many soldiers for each house depending on its size.
Our tenants had more than we did because their places
were larger. We had five. A Jewish lieutenant from Aus-
tria, two sergeants and two privates. The lieutenant spoke
Yiddish and one of the privates was of Polish extraction
and spoke good Polish. They were all very nice to my
mother and called her *Mutter.*

The lieutenant was a very handsome man in his late thir-
ties, about six feet two and close to two hundred pounds,
with gray at the temples and a beautiful smile. He seemed
like a very kind man. The two sergeants were both blond
and in their late twenties, neither one seemed very friendly. The Polish private was a short stocky man about thirty-
five with brown hair and a handlebar mustache. He was a
farmer in Germany and he liked to talk a lot. The other
private was about the same age, but taller and with a big
stomach.

They all smoked and the house was like a cloud of
smoke. They were glad I was finally home, because they
couldn't stand my mother crying while I was away with
the convoy of wagons. The Polish soldier said he would
take his horse and go to the army post in the morning to
get my wagon. They had two horses and a wagon in our
yard. The next morning I went with him and brought my
wagon home. Then I took it apart and hid the wheels in
the barn. The next day I called in a horse dealer and sold
my horse. I didn't get much but it was a great load off my
mind. This way the Germans wouldn't confiscate my horse

and they also couldn't force me to go off on another convoy.

In the house things were normal. We got along well with the Germans. The four soldiers slept on the living-room floor and the Lieutenant slept on our sofa. He ate with the officers downtown in a large house left by a Russian official. He was waiting to be transferred to officers' quarters. The Germans were not too warm toward the Austrians, even the officers, and he said he would rather stay with us but it was against regulations for officers to stay with enlisted men.

The other German soldiers got their food from the army kitchen set up in the market just as the Russians had, and then they brought it back to the house in their mess kits. Mother wouldn't let them use our dishes because their food wasn't kosher, but many times she would cook them cabbage soup or potato soup and they loved it. Father only spoke to the Lieutenant, who turned out to be well versed in the Talmud, so they had a lot in common.

In a few days the Lieutenant was transferred to officers' quarters, but he continued to come to the house to see Frumke. He took her for walks in the park or for a drive in one of the cabs. Frumke was only sixteen and a half and very pretty and the Lieutenant was more than twice her age, but it was obvious that he cared a lot for her. Frumke told me she loved him a lot but she thought she was too young to be thinking about marriage. She also told me he was a perfect gentleman.

It was late in October and our first snow had fallen. The soldiers stayed close to the house most of the time as it was cold outside and warm inside. With the Lieutenant moved out, one of the sergeants moved to the couch, the rest were still on the floor. No one knew how long it would be before they would be shipped out. Many soldiers had already been shipped out and a number of houses had been emptied of soldiers. The Lieutenant had been placed in charge of Russian prisoners, but he didn't think he would have the job for too long.

The days were very short now and the men were getting bored. Every night they smoked and played cards. The soldiers brought coffee and chocolate cookies, and Mother would prepare the samovar, and we would all drink tea or coffee. It was the first coffee we had ever tasted. On Friday nights, Mother would make chicken soup with homemade noodles, gefilte fish, chicken and potatoes. They all looked forward to Sabbath dinner with us, and the Lieutenant always came too.

The soldiers liked us and couldn't do enough for us. They chopped wood, brought in the water and filled up our barrel, they brought sugar and tea and coffee and jam. We all got along very well. The Lieutenant came to see Frumke two or three times a week. Sometimes he would discuss talmudic questions with Father, but most of the time he would go somewhere with Frumke. His name was Ezra Solander. The other four soldiers played cards every night and waited for their orders to come through. Fritz, the one with the big stomach, must have had a bad digestion system because he farted out loud a lot. Then the others would laugh and say *Auf deine Gesundheit!*

One Saturday night, Lt. Solander was at the house visiting Frumke and we were all sitting around the samovar talking and drinking tea. I got warm from the fire and from drinking tea and my eyes were burning from the soldiers' smoke, especially from Gustav the Polish soldier who was constantly puffing on his pipe, so I decided to go out for some fresh air. I used to enjoy walking around town at night.

It was a dark night but not very cold, well above freezing. I was walking on our main street, heading toward the market . . .

Lazar was still thinking of the scene he had just left at home. He was thinking especially about Frumke and the Lieutenant, wondering if they would eventually get married. From the way the Lieutenant kept coming over all the time, and from the looks passing between them, it looked serious all right. Thinking about his sister's romance reminded him of Chanka and he recalled their afternoon together in the loft. He smiled and decided he would try to get over to see Chanka next week for sure.

By this time Lazar had reached the row of saloons across from the market and he could hear German soldiers singing drinking songs inside. He stopped in front of the one near the corner and stood under the streetlight listening to the words. German is so close to Yiddish, he thought, it would probably be easy to learn. As long as the Germans were going to be around for a while, and it was beginning to look like they were here to stay, it might help to get a good job if he learned to speak German.

He tried to look inside the saloon, but the windows were fogged and all he could make out were the dark forms of people moving around just inside. Yes, he decided, it would be a good idea to learn the language and he would start right away. The song ended with a loud cheer and Lazar continued slowly down the street, practicing the words of the song.

The door of the saloon opened behind him and the sound of a woman's shrill laughter spilled out into the night. Lazar glanced back and saw that a German soldier had emerged from the saloon. Standing unsteadily under the streetlight for a moment, the soldier looked up and down the street, then turned and started walking in Lazar's direction. Probably heading for the army post to sleep it off, Lazar thought. Drunken soldiers were no novelty in Volkovysk on a Saturday night these days.

The image Lazar had of the soldier standing under the streetlight was of a short middle-aged man of medium build with a thick squared-off mustache, an enlisted man with his tunic unbuttoned. As he continued to stroll along, Lazar could hear the soldier walking behind him, stumbling occasionally and muttering to himself. When Lazar reached the saloon in the middle of the block he paused, listening to the words of another drinking song even more boisterous than the last, and he forgot all about the drunken soldier behind him.

Suddenly, a hand gripped his neck from behind, spun him to the left and propelled him around behind the saloon! He twisted his head and saw that it was the German soldier, and he tried to pull away but the grip on his neck was like iron! He heard the soldier muttering to himself, "Warte nur, mein zartes junges Hünchen, gleich wirst du meine steife deutsche Rübe in deinem russischen Aschloch fühlen, eh?" but he could make no sense of it!

Lazar was cold with fear. There was no time to think, everything was happening so quickly. What did the soldier want? Over and over Lazar asked in Yiddish: Vus machts du? Vus machts du? but the soldier just laughed and said "Mein Lieber, du wirst schon sehen was für ein saftiges Geshonk ich für dich habe. Es wird dir gefallen!" The soldier's speech was guttural and the words were so slurred that Lazar couldn't understand what he was saying, but the tone was so frightening that he renewed his struggling, trying to get away. It was no use, the soldier was too strong.

With his hand still gripping Lazar's neck, the soldier pushed him inside the dark storage shack behind the saloon and forced him to the floor on his stomach. Lazar's heart was pounding wildly. He writhed and twisted, kicking and lashing out, but he couldn't get away! The sol-

81

dier's hand gripped his neck like a vise and his forearm bore down on Lazar's back, pinning him to the floor. Vus machts du! Vus machts du! It was no longer a question, but a plea! The soldier only grunted. There was a smell of cabbage and stale cigar and vodka on his breath. Lazar felt his pants being yanked down and the soldier's other hand grabbed his hip. Vus machts du! Vus machts du!

Suddenly he felt something big and hard pushing into his rectum and he screamed out in blinding pain. The soldier's hand let go of his neck and wrapped around his face, covering his mouth and stifling the scream. It felt like a hot poker was being pushed in and out, in and out, and Lazar saw flashes of color in the dark shack as he tried to scream out and instead choked on his own saliva. The German's face was next to his now, as he lay heavily on Lazar's back, sweat pouring from his face, grunting and muttering as he thrust faster and faster into Lazar. The pain was excruciating, sharp searing jabs that raced through his lower back and stomach, he couldn't stand it! Oh, God! Oh, God!

And then it was over. The soldier gave one last long thrust, groaned, and rolled slowly off Lazar, releasing his grip. Lazar felt warm liquid running down the inside of his thighs. The pain was unbearable and it still felt like something was inside him. He was sobbing uncontrollably. Then he felt sick to his stomach and vomited on the floor. On his knees now, sobbing and retching in the dark, he heard the soldier get up and stumble from the shack.

After a while, the waves of nausea and pain subsided enough for Lazar to pull up his pants and stagger outside. Dazed and shaking, he leaned against the side of the saloon and breathed deeply until the cool night air cleared the dizziness and he managed to stop shaking. Then slowly, painfully, he made his way home through the deserted streets. There was no sign of the German soldier.

ק

*He entered the house quietly and at first no one noticed
him standing in the doorway. All he wanted to do was get
into bed and crawl under the covers with Rosetka. He was
still in pain and his head was throbbing and he just didn't
want to talk to anybody right now because he felt very
ashamed. His mother and father were already in the bedroom and that was a break. The others were still at the
table, talking quietly and sipping tea. Maybe he could sneak
in without their noticing him. He tried to close the door
without making a noise, but his sister heard something,
turned, took one look at him and turned white as a sheet.*

"Lazar, what's wrong! What happened to you!"

*The others turned to see what she was staring at and now
they were all looking at him. He started to cry again and
hobbled into the kitchen so they wouldn't see. Frumke and
the Lieutenant got up and hurried after him. Frumke
asked again what happened, but Lazar couldn't stop crying.*

*"Now, Lazar," the Lieutenant said gently, "you must
stop crying and you must tell us exactly what has happened so we will know how to help you, do you understand? You are a brave young man, not a little boy, so
there's no need to cry. Come now, tell us what happened."*

*And Lazar sobbed out the whole story. When he came to
the part about what happened in the shack, Frumke
turned away and started to cry and the Lieutenant banged
his fist into his hand in anger.*

"Fritz! Gustav! Heinz! Werner! Get in here!"

*The soldiers came running into the kitchen. Quietly, the
Lieutenant repeated the story. They too were furious. Gustav went over to Lazar, put an arm around his shoulder
and asked softly in Polish, "Did you get a good look at
him, Lazar? Would you be able to point him out to us if
you saw him again?"*

83

Lazar nodded. They waited while he washed and changed his clothes. Frumke had stopped crying and hovered over him, buttoning his shirt because his hands were shaking too much to do it himself. The soldiers talked among themselves in hushed voices.

"If we find the bastard, I'll beat the hell out of him!"

"No, he should be court-martialed."

"What the hell, all they'll do is ship him to the Front. That's too good for him, he may not catch a bullet."

"Ja, what we should do is cut it off for him!"

"What we will do," the Lieutenant said firmly, "is I will place him under arrest and you will hold him for me until the military police arrive. And that's all we will do, understood?"

Lazar was ready. He felt a little better, especially with the Lieutenant taking charge.

"Frumke, you'd better stay here, dear," the Lieutenant said in Yiddish. "And there's no need to discuss this with your parents until the morning, it would only upset them. Don't worry about Lazar, we'll watch out for him. I'll be back soon."

It didn't take long. In the third saloon they came to, Lazar spotted the soldier who had raped him, sitting in a back corner and drinking alone. There was no mistaking that mustache and his tunic was still unbuttoned.

"That's him! That's him!" Lazar screamed, pointing at the soldier. The singing died out and the saloon was suddenly very quiet. The soldier made an effort to get up, but the two sergeants were already on him, each grabbing him by an arm, and they threw him back down in his chair with such force that he went over backward and landed on the floor. The Lieutenant stood over him, announcing loudly that he was under arrest. The other two had already gone for the military police.

Lazar was still standing just inside the door, screaming hysterically over and over again, "That's him! That's him!" until he suddenly felt very hot and dizzy and the next thing he knew he was home again, in bed with a cold cloth on his forehead and Frumke sitting by the bed holding his hand.

. . . It was a long time before I overcame the fear of that incident. My behind was sore for days afterward. The next day two military police took me to their headquarters to identify the soldier and tell what happened. Lieutenant Solander and the two sergeants were with me and the Lieutenant interpreted everything for me in Yiddish so I could understand.

The soldier finally admitted raping me. The head officer said the German Army was very sorry for what happened to me and asked if I wanted to see a doctor. I said no, I just wanted to go home, so they let me go home then. Later, when our two sergeants came home, they told us that the soldier had been taken to the stockade after the trial and was to be shipped to the Front.

Frankly, as I am writing this incident, believe it or not I still get shivers going through me. At that age I never knew of such things as homosexuals. As far as I knew, sex takes place between a man and woman when they are married, or sometimes before marriage like with Joe and Katanya, but that's all I knew. That incident left me with a very strange feeling inside me about sex and I shied away from it for a long time afterward.

3. ✌

It was a cold hard winter and the snow had piled high. Our soldiers had been transferred to nearby villages to take over the farms which had been abandoned when the big landowners fled to Moscow, all except Gustav Danchek, the Polish soldier, who had been put in charge of the Rittmeister's stable. Herr Rittmeister was the officer in charge of all the farms and he lived with his staff in a big white house about one kilometer from our house.

Lt. Solander had received orders to rejoin his unit on the front lines. Before that, he had asked Frumke to marry him, and Father, who liked him and enjoyed their talmudic discussions, had no objection, but Mother told Frumke she would not allow it because Frumke was too young and because Ezra was a soldier and who knew what could happen to a soldier in a war? When he came to say good-bye, he said that if Frumke was still not married after the war, he would come back for her. I was sad to see him go, I liked him. So did Frumke, but she told me she never intended to marry him because he was too old for her and she was too young to get married anyway.

The economy in Volkovysk was very bad. There were shortages of practically everything. The trains still weren't running and merchants had to depend on horse and wagon for transportation to Bialystok for their merchandise. That took several days and even then the wholesalers in Bialystok were running out of goods too, so the trip might be for nothing.

Then the Germans issued an order that Russian money had to be exchanged for German Marks or scrip, that unless we did that our money would be no good. No one liked the scrip, but the military government said that as soon as they received more Marks, the scrip could be exchanged. In the meantime, they ordered all merchants to accept scrip.

The Germans were very well organized and we all cooperated with the German authorities. Our merchants started to operate their businesses as usual and the peasants came to market as before, selling whatever they had to sell. No one was afraid of the Germans. We had respect for them and they had respect for us.

In spite of the cold weather, work continued on rebuilding the army post and repairing the railroad. The Germans used the captured Russian soldiers to do most of the work, but in addition they ordered everybody to work one day a week without pay. My day was Tuesday. In the second week in November, I was working at the damaged railroad bridge and accidentally fell into the edge of the river. The water was ice cold and my clothes started to freeze and stiffen, so I asked the sergeant in charge if I could go home but he wouldn't let me. That night I had a high fever and I was sick in bed for a week.

The following Tuesday I reported to work with a note from Dr. Weiner and I gave it to the officer in charge. He couldn't believe that the sergeant had refused to let me go home. He asked me how old I was and when I told him I was eleven and a half, he said, *"Du bist zu jung!"* and he sent me home, so for the rest of the winter I didn't have to work the one day a week for no pay. But there were no jobs for me and all that was coming in was a little rent money. Luckily we had Belka, so we were able to sell some milk, butter and cheese. Many of our neighbors were less fortunate and we helped them all we could. Sometimes they even asked for our potato peelings, but we gave them potatoes instead. It was a good thing we had so many potatoes stored away for the winter.

Everybody patiently waited for spring to arrive, hoping the railroad would start up again and the economy would get better. Meanwhile, I learned to speak German very well, almost without an accent, although I still couldn't read or write it. The fighting was now well to the east of

Slonim and we no longer heard the guns at night. As the weather grew milder and the farmers began to spread manure on their fields, the German Government started to buy horses, cows and chickens to replenish the abandoned farms and it was obvious they intended to get them running again.

Early in April I went to visit Gustav at the stable. He was glad to see me and showed me around. He had a two-room apartment next to the stable with a small kitchen where he could make coffee or tea. He ate his meals in the big house with the rest of the staff. Herr Rittmeister had his own private dining room. There were three woman cooks and four housemaids. Everybody seemed to be living very comfortably there.

Gustav asked me how things were going and I said that Father continued to get worse and there wasn't much we could do, and that I wanted to work to earn money for the house but there didn't seem to be any jobs.

Gustav took me to see the Feldwebel, his boss, who did the hiring for the farms. I spoke to the Feldwebel in German and he was impressed. I told him I could handle horses because I had owned my own and that I was sure I would be good on a farm. Gustav added that I would be a good interpreter with the peasants. That seemed to convince the Feldwebel and I was hired. He told me to report on Tuesday when the soldiers drove in from the farms to pick up supplies and he would assign me then.

I explained that I couldn't work on the Sabbath and he said I could make that arrangement with the head man on the farm. I also told him that I didn't want to be located too far from my home and he said he knew a farm where he could assign me that would be all right. I knew the farm, it was about fifteen kilometers from Volkovysk. Then the

Feldwebel gave me a paper to sign. I was happy to get the job.

I ran home to tell my parents the good news. They didn't approve. They told me I couldn't go because I was only twelve and the work would be too hard, and also that I would have to eat nonkosher food. I promised I wouldn't eat what I wasn't supposed to, but my father was upset and said I was turning into a goy. I didn't want to upset my father. I tried to reason with him. I said we needed the money and if the work was too hard, I would quit. Finally I told them I had already signed the paper and it was too late to back out now. By this time Mother and Frumke were both crying, but my mind was made up and at last my parents said all right.

Tuesday, 4 May 1915, I reported for work at the Feldwebel's office. In the afternoon I was assigned to the farm and introduced to the sergeant in charge of the farm. He told me to help load the wagon and then we left for the farm. It took us two hours to make the trip and we arrived just as it was getting dark. This was the first time I had ever been away from home alone before, except for weekends at Joe's house, and I wondered what it would be like to be on my own. It didn't take long to find out.

Chapter Five

1. ✌

Lazar lay on the floor on his makeshift bed of straw in the dark and cried. It was one thing to act like a man when adults were around and to be brave and responsible, but it was another to be alone on a strange farm with five German soldiers up in the main house playing cards and drinking schnapps, while he had to stay down here shivering in the dark under one thin blanket in a one-room shack with broken windows and no furniture and no lights, and he could swear there was somebody or something walking around out there in the woods! He had told the Sergeant after dinner that maybe it was escaped Russian prisoners who hid during the day and foraged for food at night, but the Sergeant had told him to ignore it and go to sleep.

He didn't like the Sergeant. He was a stern man, always frowning behind his steel-rimmed glasses as though Lazar had done something wrong. The others seemed all right, but it was the Sergeant who gave the orders and he wasn't very pleasant about it. In fact, that's all the Sergeant seemed to do, give Lazar orders. Unload the wagon, boy. Get straw and make yourself a bed in one of the shacks, boy. Eat your dinner when we're finished eating, then clean up the kitchen and go to sleep. Tomorrow, get up at five, take care of the horses, come here for breakfast, then I'll tell you what to do.

No please or do you mind or would you, just do this! do that! No bed with a mattress and soft pillow and snug quilt. No warm fire, no Rosetka to snuggle up to him and lick his face. No mother and father and sister to love him, no potato soup and fresh black bread. Dinner had been awful, cooked by one of the soldiers. Some kind of watery soup, stale bread and dry jelly. He wasn't even allowed to eat with the soldiers or sleep in the main house. Verboten, the Sergeant said. What had he gotten himself into? Dishes! They made him do dishes like a kitchenmaid! Lazar was cold and uncomfortable and unhappy and he wished he was home.

What was that? Lazar stopped crying and held his breath, listening. It wasn't the noise he had heard before in the woods, nor even the crickets outside. It was closer. Something was inside the shack. Lazar strained in the dark, trying to identify the sound. Rats! Oh god, there were rats scurrying across the room! Shuddering, Lazar listened to the sound of their feet scratching on the wooden floor near him and panicked. He leaped to his feet, ran blindly out of the shack, and raced up the hill to the main house as fast as he could.

The soldiers were still at the table playing cards and drinking. As Lazar burst through the door and ran into the room, the Sergeant looked up from his cards, glowering.

"Was ist los?"

"Rats, Sergeant, there are rats in my room!"

"Was erwartest du von mir?"

"Please, Sergeant, I'm scared of rats! Can't I sleep here in the house tonight? Anywhere, I'll sleep on the floor! Please, Sergeant, please!" Lazar fought back the tears. He didn't

want to cry in front of these soldiers no matter what.

"Nein!" roared the Sergeant, banging his fist on the table. "Est ist verboten, im hause zu schlafen!"

But Lazar was more frightened by the thought of returning to the shack than he was by the Sergeant's tone and he stood his ground. Looking around, he noticed a small space above the oven in the corner. It looked large enough for Lazar and it would surely be warmer and safer sleeping there than in the shack with the rats.

He begged the Sergeant to let him sleep in the space above the oven where he would be quiet, he promised, and would be in no one's way. One of the soldiers leaned toward the Sergeant and in a low voice said, "Lass das arme Kind herein, es hat Angst." Let the poor kid in, he's scared. Lazar understood and cast a pleading look at the Sergeant. Finally, the Sergeant shrugged and turned back to his cards. The other soldier smiled at Lazar, nodded and motioned with his head toward the space Lazar had picked out for a bed.

It was getting late. The soldiers ended the card game and went to bed. One of them tossed Lazar a blanket and he crawled up into his "bed." It was cramped quarters. On his back, the space barely accommodated his torso and he was forced to dangle his legs over the edge. It was better on his side, at least he could curl up in a fetal position and be fairly comfortable, but whenever he shifted position he banged his head on the rafter just above.

By this time he was overtired and had difficulty falling asleep. The space was really too small for him, but it was warm and safe, like a little cave, and eventually he simply cried himself to sleep.

Lazar opened his eyes. It was still dark and for a moment he was disoriented, thinking he was home in his own bed, but when he sat up and banged his head on the rafter he remembered where he was. He crawled out of his cubicle above the stove and slid to the floor, for the first time in hours able to stretch. It seemed that every muscle in his body ached.

The soldiers were still sleeping. He groped his way through the house and outside. It would be light soon and he wanted to make a good impression on the Sergeant by having his chores done before breakfast. As he cleaned out the stalls and fed the horses, his aches and pains gradually faded and his spirits picked up. This wouldn't be so bad, he thought. After all, he really liked working on a farm, taking care of horses and growing things, and two and a half Marks a day would come in handy at home. Maybe he could even get a couple boys in town to join him on the farm and then he would have company. That's a great idea, he thought, he would mention it to the Sergeant at breakfast. By the time he was done, washed and on his way back to the house, the sun was coming up and Lazar was whistling.

The Sergeant was in the kitchen pouring himself some coffee, the other soldiers were in the next room having breakfast.

"Well," said the Sergeant, smiling, "how did you like your bed last night?"

"It was terrible, but it was still better than being alone in that other house with the rats."

The Sergeant laughed. "You will have to sleep there sooner or later, you know."

"Yes, but I had an idea this morning, Sergeant. When we go into town for supplies, I will try to get a couple more boys to sign up to work here. Then you will have more help on the farm and I will have company and I won't mind sleeping down there because I won't be alone. What do you think of that idea, Sergeant?"

The Sergeant scowled. "I said nothing about you going with me for supplies. Es ist verboten! You will stay here and work; I will go to town alone."

"But, Sergeant, I have to go home! I have a sick father, I have to see him. It was agreed with Herr Feldwebel when I signed the paper!" Lazar was getting excited. This Sergeant was a mean man! After sleeping all night in a hole with his legs hanging out, getting up in the dark and cleaning the whole stable before breakfast, this was his reward? He wouldn't stay here, that's what! "I won't stay here, I'll quit! You can't make me stay here and work if I don't want to! I'll run away if you don't let me go to town with you and visit my family and my sick father!"

Lazar was close to tears. It was the first time he had ever yelled at an adult, least of all a German sergeant, but he didn't care, even if the Sergeant hit him he wasn't going to stand for this, it just wasn't fair! But the Sergeant ignored Lazar's tantrum, he just told him to eat his breakfast and get ready for work. When Lazar refused the bacon because it was not kosher, the Sergeant laughed again and joined the others in the next room.

He sat at the kitchen table, chewing his breakfast furiously, still upset by what the Sergeant had said, but then he heard one of the soldiers telling the Sergeant to "ease up on him, he's only a boy." Lazar nodded to himself, agreeing with the soldier. Right, I'm only a boy! There were times when being "only a boy" had its advantages. Lazar smiled. He knew then that it was going to be all right. He would go into town on his own terms. The Sergeant had a loud bark, that was all. Lazar would learn to handle the Sergeant. Who could resist a boy who worked like a man?

. . . After breakfast, the Sergeant asked me if I knew how to plow. I said yes. He told me to take two horses and a plow and he showed me where to start. The truth is I never plowed before in my life, but I had watched our neighbor plow and it didn't look that hard.

It was a lot harder than it looked. I had trouble keeping the horses in line and the plow was bigger than I was. The handlebars were up to my chin and every time the plow struck a rock, the bars would hit my chin and knock me down. Then the horses would get off line, dragging the plow away, and I would have to run to catch up and stop them. It's a good thing the Sergeant wasn't watching. It took me half the morning to learn how to plow a straight line.

It was a long hard day and I was glad to see it end. By time I took care of the horses and washed up, I was really hungry. When I walked into the kitchen, I got a surprise. There was a woman serving dinner to the soldiers! I ate with her in the kitchen and she told me she had just been hired to cook and clean house, which meant I wouldn't have to do the dishes or get the fire started in the morning, and that I wouldn't have to eat the soldier's cooking which wasn't very good. I was delighted.

Her name was Kristina. She was about forty-five, a little on the heavy side with long brown hair tied in a pigtail. She was a widow and lived on a small farm down the road with a son nineteen, a daughter seventeen, and another daughter who was fourteen. At night when she was finished with her work, she would either walk home or her son would pick her up with the wagon. I liked it because for one thing I ate better and for another I had somebody to talk to in Russian, instead of German all the time.

Everything was under way now on the farm. In the mornings the Sergeant went to the nearby villages and hired men and women to work for the day. I continued the plowing and harrowing for several days. Then we planted the summer grain and potatoes and a big garden with all kinds of vegetables. I didn't mind the days, but I hated the nights crammed into the cubbyhole over the stove.

Usually I was the first one up in the morning, but one day I overslept and Kristina cried when she found me in that hole with my legs dangling over the edge. She thought it was very mean of the Germans to make me sleep like that, but I told her not to talk to them about it because it was still better than sleeping in the other house. She wanted me to sleep at her farm, but I told her about my plan to get some other boys and then we would fix up one of the houses for ourselves and everything would be all right. I must say she took care of me like a mother and always saw that I had plenty of food when the soldiers weren't looking.

The second Tuesday finally came and sure enough the Sergeant let me come along. He gave me my first pay voucher for thirty-five Marks, which I turned in at the main office and received the money. Kristina had also given me a half bag of flour to take home to my mother. We got to town about noon and the Sergeant told me to be back by three o'clock. My parents were very happy to see me and wanted to know all about my work. I told them that I liked the work and that everything was fine. Then I had lunch and rushed back to town to see if I could get a few boys. I managed to convince two boys to come with me and I took them to the office so they could sign up. I told them to be back by three o'clock and I went home again for two hours with my family.

Mother and Frumke tried to convince me not to go back to the farm, but I said we needed the money and the summer would pass quickly. Father hardly spoke. He didn't look well at all. It seemed to me that he had lost interest in living. I told him that I knew the food I was eating wasn't kosher, but that at least I wasn't eating the pork or ham and I wasn't working on the Sabbath. I don't think he believed me, but he didn't say anything. I gave Mother the money and told her not to worry about me, I could take care of myself. Frumke was angry with me for not staying home and she went into the kitchen so she wouldn't have to kiss me good-bye. I felt bad about leaving, but there was nothing I could do.

When I got to the main office, there was no sign of the two boys. The wagon was loaded and the Sergeant was ready to leave. I didn't know what to do. I couldn't picture going back alone and sleeping in that hole again. I begged the Sergeant to wait a few minutes, maybe they would show up. We waited about ten minutes and just as the Sergeant was about to leave, the two boys came running down the street with small packs on their backs, waving to me. I was really happy to see them. We all got into the wagon and took off, arriving at the farm just before dark.

Kristina was there waiting for us. She was very happy to see the two boys with me because now I wouldn't have to sleep in the hole anymore. We fixed up some straw for beds after we unloaded the wagon, there wasn't much more we could do until the next day. Then we got our supper. I asked my boss if we could take a couple hours in the morning to fix up our room after we cleaned the stable, and he said yes. He said: *Mach schnell!* and I said: *Jawohl, mein Herr!* I was beginning to think he liked me. He even thanked me for getting the two boys to come and work on the farm!

The first night the three of us slept on the floor, which wasn't what my two pals had pictured. Thank god there was no sign of the rats. I told them they would like it better after a few days, especially after we fixed up the room. They were each about two years older than me. The next morning after we cleaned the stable, we worked on the

97

room. There was plenty of lumber and we made a platform for the three of us to sleep on and a table and a bench to eat on. We took empty flour bags and stuffed them with straw for pillows. The Sergeant gave us some blankets and I had brought a lamp and some candles. It wasn't like home, but I was happy because I wasn't alone.

We ate lunch and went to work. At the end of the day, we washed up and took our dinner to our room. My new friends were disappointed with the place and the work and they started to blame me for talking them into coming. I told them I didn't lie to them, it was as I had told them, and I reminded them that they told me they needed the money because there was no work for them in Volkovysk. Anyway, I said, if it's good enough for me, it's good enough for you. Where else could they make two and a half Marks a day plus room and board? That seemed to satisfy them for a while.

But after a week or so, they started to complain to me again. This time they complained that I was bossing them too much and making them work too hard. That really made me mad. I told them I worked twice as hard as they did and the only reason I told them what to do was because I spoke German and the Sergeant told me what to tell them. I said Kristina gives us more food than we can eat, we have our own place to stay, we get two and a half Marks a day and we don't have to work on Sabbath, what more do you want? I said I don't get paid any more than you do and I don't see any reason for you to complain. Then I said they should go to sleep because we had work to do in the morning, and I put out the light.

In the morning they told me they were sorry about complaining the night before, it was just that they were a little blue. I didn't tell them, but they had scared the hell out of me. I could just see them quitting and leaving me alone to do all the work and to sleep there alone, because I wouldn't go back to sleeping in that hole again no matter what. I had just about decided that if they quit, I would too. Now I was glad that for the moment they seemed satisfied to stay.

I got the horse and wagon ready for my boss and me and we went to the village to hire some peasants for the day. We were able to get ten men and five women. Breakfast was ready when we got back and by time we finished eating, all of the peasants arrived. We finished the planting that day and the next day we started cutting hay. We had to cut several acres by hand, but the sun was shining and it wasn't too hot, just the right kind of day for making hay.

It took several days to get the first cutting down. When the sun is out, it doesn't take long for the top to dry and then the hay has to be turned. We did have a horse-drawn turner and rake and I showed my friends how to use it. In a few days the hay was dry and we started loading it into wagons and taking it to the barn. In a week we had all the hay under roof. I loved the smell of new hay. Even my buddies were in a better frame of mind, now that they had their own horse and wagon to work with.

Two weeks had passed. The Sergeant got word that the three younger soldiers were being transferred and probably shipped to the Front. I asked him how the war was going and he said he didn't know, but the German lines were somewhere not too far east of Slonim which meant their advance had slowed down. The Sergeant told me to get the wagon ready to go into town. He wasn't very happy about losing three of his five soldiers. Since all the planting was done and the hay was cut, I asked if my two friends could go into town with us and he said yes.

We got to the city about eleven, reported to the paymaster's office for our pay, and then had until three o'clock before we had to be back. I was worried that maybe the other two wouldn't report back, but I tried not to think about it. I just wanted to get home and see my family . . .

Lazar slowed to a walk. For some reason he was in no great hurry to get home. Everything seemed just a bit strange. Familiar but strange. With the exception of the few hours at home last time in for supplies, he had now been on the farm for five weeks. It had become "his place." Moishe and Boris, the Sergeant, the soldiers, Kristina, they weren't family but he did spend every day with them now and they were no longer strangers.

Not that Mother and Father and Frumke weren't still his family, of course they were, and of course he still loved them dearly, but he was feeling a little strange this time. It may have had to do with the shortness of these visits. Probably if he were to stay a day or two, instead of only a few hours, he would feel less out of place, more like he still belonged instead of just visiting. He also felt less sure of himself at home. On the farm, he was practically the Sergeant's assistant, interpreting in the villages, taking charge of the stable, doing a man's work in the fields. At home he felt like the baby.

Well, it wouldn't do to think too much about these things, he decided. It was only for a few hours and anyway he was really looking forward to seeing everybody and telling them about life on the farm. As he turned into the yard, he quickened his pace and headed for the house. Frumke was just outside the front door and saw him come through the gate. She waved, then yelled into the house:

"Mother! Father! Lazar's home!"

But the next few hours were even more difficult than Lazar had anticipated. Father was ill again and had been confined to his bed for the past two weeks. He didn't look at all well. Lazar sat by his father's bed and told him all about the farm and his work, eliminating any of the bad parts of course. His mother and sister sat just outside the bedroom, listening to Lazar talk, but not wishing to intrude on the boy's visit with his father.

After nearly an hour, Lazar's father smiled and said, "You know, I think I'll get up and have lunch with you. I feel a little better."

He was weak when he stood up and he leaned on Lazar for support. He reached over and felt Lazar's shoulder with his free hand, admiring his son's new muscles, and he said with a wistful smile, "My little mensch, you're growing up." Then he bent over and kissed Lazar on the cheek. Lazar's eyes filled with tears. It was the first time his father had kissed him in a long, long time.

He walked with his father to the table and his father sat down in his usual seat. Frumke set the table. Lazar went into the kitchen to tell his mother that Father was feeling better and had decided to get up to have lunch with them. Before he could finish, his mother grabbed his face between her hands and said, "God bless you, Layshkela, for coming home and putting new strength in your father's heart!" Then her eyes filled with tears too.

It was too much for Lazar to handle. He mumbled that he would be back in a minute, he wanted to go see Belka, then he ran out to the barn and cried. He didn't even know why he was crying, he was simply so full of emotion— guilt for the thoughts he was having on the way home; love for his parents; sadness for his father because deep down he had the feeling his father was dying; loneliness for what once was and could no longer be, to be the baby once more, without responsibilities, as far back as Lazar could remember he had worked and he had felt these great responsibilities—it was all bottled up inside and it needed to get out.

"Oh God, dear God, please help my father get well and don't let him suffer so much!"

Frumke had come into the barn to see what was the matter. Belka was at pasture, so she knew that Lazar couldn't have come to the barn to see the cow. When she found him crying and heard him praying out loud, she waited until he was finished and then put her arm around him to comfort him.

"Everything will be all right, Lazar, don't worry. Your money paid for the doctor and the medicine, you should be proud. Besides, see how much better he feels now that you're here. Now come on, wash your face and come to lunch, he's asking for you."

At lunch, Lazar sat in his usual seat on his father's left and continued his discourse on life at the farm, as he ate his mother's soup. From time to time his father nodded and smiled over at his mother. The boy's growing up, he seemed to be saying, he's not a baby anymore. But to his mother he was still her baby and she decided to bake him some babka to take back with him. After lunch, Lazar's father announced that he felt well enough to sit up until it was time for Lazar to leave. For the next hour Lazar cleaned out the barn and gave Rosetka and her son a bath. It helped to keep busy.

At two-thirty he kissed his family, said he would see them in two weeks and not to worry, and with the freshly baked babka in a bag, left to rejoin his group, wondering again if the boys would be there. He wouldn't blame them if they didn't show up, he was that tempted to stay home himself, and would have too if not for the money. This business of being two different people in two different places wasn't easy.

But the boys were there waiting and so was the Sergeant,

the wagon already loaded, and soon they were all on the road back to the farm where Kristina would have a hot meal waiting. Lazar put his family away for another two weeks and thought about the work he would do tomorrow.

2. ♄

When I first went to work on the farm, my boss was like a tiger. He never had a kind or friendly word to say to anyone. As time went on he seemed to become a little more considerate of people, especially when he lost the three soldiers and had to depend more on other people.

One day the Sergeant was writing at his desk and he asked me to come in and sit beside him. It was the first time he ever called me into his office. He told me he was writing a letter to his family and I reminded him of his twelve-year-old son. He showed me a picture of his family, his wife, two sons, twelve and eight, and a daughter who was five. They were all good-looking and I told him so. I could see tears in his eyes.

His wife was a slender woman with short blond hair and the children were also blond. The sons looked like him and the daughter looked like his wife. There was something written on the bottom of the picture, but I couldn't read German so I asked him to read it.

Meinem Hermann mit meiner ganzen Liebe. To my Hermann with all my love. I told him: *Sie müssen sehr stolz auf sie sein*, you must be very proud of them. *Ja*, he said and he looked out the window for a long time. Then he told me what work he wanted me and the boys to do and that was the end of the conversation.

It was the end of the third week in August. We had one group of peasants cutting the second crop of hay while the three of us brought the dry hay into the barn, and another group was threshing and bagging oats. My boss rounded up a number of wagons to take the oats to the warehouse in Volkovysk, from which they would be shipped to Germany. I asked if I could go into town with one of the wagons so I could see my family, but he wouldn't allow me to go because he said there was too much work to be done on the farm. He said I would have to wait until the second Tuesday in September.

I didn't like it. I told him it was over three weeks since we were in town and the other boys were complaining too. And I told him we needed our pay. He said if Boris and Moishe don't like it, they can quit and walk home! He hadn't yelled like that in a long time and I got scared, but I didn't tell my friends about it for fear they would leave. I just told them when he said we could go and that then we would have a really big pay. That seemed to appeal to them and they didn't complain.

For the next week or so we got ten acres ready for sowing winter wheat and we began to plow up the early potatoes. I went into the house early one afternoon to ask the Sergeant something. I was in the kitchen getting a glass of water and they must have heard me. Kristina came out of the bedroom buttoning her blouse. Her hair was all messed up and when she saw me watching her, she tried to straighten it and her face got red. She asked me what I wanted and I told her I wanted to talk to the Sergeant. She said he was sleeping and I should come back later.

Kristina was a young widow and Hermann was away from his wife for three years. I don't know what they were doing but I could guess. I didn't see anything wrong with it, but for the next few days Kristina cooked up a storm and she blushed whenever she saw me. Even the Sergeant seemed a little more relaxed toward me for a while.

On the second Monday in September, the Sergeant told me he had received orders to prepare an additional ten acres of winter wheat and that meant we would not be able to go to town the next day. He promised we could go the following Tuesday no matter what. The three of us were very disappointed, but there didn't seem anything we could do about it unless we ran away, and if we did that we would lose our pay for five weeks. We talked it over in our room and decided to stay.

That Thursday we had a heavy rain and we couldn't work in the fields, so the Sergeant told me the three of us should work in the shed chopping wood for the winter. We had to saw the logs into smaller sections and then split them with an ax. We took turns, two of us on the saw and one on the ax. It was my turn to use the ax . . .

It was a big ax, too big for Lazar, though he would never admit it even to himself. It was fun to split logs. There was a peasant who came to his house each year to do the wood for the winter and he had watched him split wood for a whole afternoon once, fascinated by the way the ax seemed to hum through the air and strike the log with a loud ping *at just the right spot, cutting cleanly through the log and ending with a* thunk *into the big chopping block as the two halves of the log would slowly topple over, one to each side, and fall to the ground.*

Imitating the peasant's stance, Lazar spread his legs wide, spit on his hands and grabbed the handle about fifteen centimeters from the end. He took a deep breath and swung the ax in a slow arc that came down on the end of the log, well off center, sending a small wedge flying to the side and leaving the log teetering on the chopping block, the blade of the ax sunk into the block next to the log. Pulling the blade from the block, Lazar repeated the motion, this time succeeding in striking the log in the center but not with sufficient force to split it. Now the ax blade was stuck midway through the log and Lazar's hands were stinging from the incomplete blow.

Embarrassed, he glanced over his shoulder to see if Boris and Moishe were watching. They were a split second ahead of him and had already turned back to their work, but from the way they were now feverishly sawing away with ridiculous grins on their faces, he was certain they had been watching him. He'd show them this time! He worked the blade loose, steadied the log on the block, spit on his hands again, and this time he swung the ax higher and harder, determined to split the log in one clean blow.

But somehow Lazar missed the log altogether, the side of the blade glancing off the side of the chopping block and continuing downward to strike Lazar on the inside of his right foot. He yelled out in pain, dropped the ax and looked down at his foot. The blade had cut cleanly through his boot just at the arch and blood was beginning to flow through the cut in the boot and onto the ground.

The boys were already at his side. Boris went running toward the house to get the Sergeant. Moishe helped Lazar sit down and get his boot and stocking off. It looked like a deep cut and was bleeding heavily. Lazar was crying now and Moishe tried to calm him down. Boris came running back, out of breath.

"The Sergeant says he's too busy to come. He says to wash it with cold water and put a bandage on it. He says . . ."

"Where are we supposed to get a bandage? Where's the water? Where's Kristina?" Lazar asked between sobs.

Just then Kristina came running up to the shed, bandage and cloth tucked under her arm and a pan of water in her hands, the water sloshing over the edge as she ran.

"Out of the way, boys, let Kristina have a look!" she said

*as she put the pan of water down, handed Boris the ban-
dage and cloth, and leaned over to examine Lazar's foot.
"Don't cry, dear, Kristina's here and she'll make it better,
don't worry. It's not the first cut she's had to fix, you know.
I'm an old hand at this. And don't worry, accidents happen even to the best of men. It doesn't look so bad, we'll
just wash it off and stop the bleeding."*

*As she talked, rapidly and in a soft voice, she put Lazar's
foot into the water and with a small cloth began to wipe
gently around the cut. The pan of water turned first pink
and then a dark red from Lazar's blood. Kristina took the
clean towel that was draped over her shoulder and she
wrapped Lazar's foot with it. Then she held the wrapped
foot in her lap and pressed firmly over the wound to stop
the bleeding, all the time continuing her steady stream of
chatter, which eventually had the desired effect of calming Lazar. It was obvious that Kristina had been through
this many times before on her own farm.*

*When the bleeding finally stopped, she neatly ban-
daged the wound and stood up. Smiling, she helped Lazar
up. He put his weight on the bandaged foot, gingerly at
first and then, when there was no pain, all the way.*

*"I'm all right now. Spasibo, Kristina, thank you for
helping me. I'll put my boot on and go back to work. It
feels fine."*

*"Are you sure, child? Perhaps you should rest today. I
can tell Hermann . . . the Sergeant . . . to let you . . ."*

"No! I'm okay, really. Don't tell him anything."

*Kristina shrugged, picked up the pan and headed back
to the house, shaking her head and mumbling to herself
about stubborn boys who want to act like stubborn men.
Lazar put his boot back on. It was a little tight because of
the bandage, but his foot didn't hurt much now, only a
sort of dull pain, and he was determined not to let it inter-
fere. If the Sergeant didn't think it was important enough*

to come and look at, he wasn't going to give him the satis-
faction of acting like a baby and asking for time off. He
told Boris to take over with the ax and for the rest of the
day Lazar sawed wood with Moishe.

By the end of the day it started to throb and was very
painful. My buddies got our dinner and I went to our
room. The Sergeant didn't come over to see me. I struggled to get my boot off because now my foot was swollen.
After dinner Kristina came over and brought boiled water
and salt and told me to soak my foot in it. The swelling
didn't go down, but after a while the throbbing stopped
and I bandaged it again with a clean bandage Kristina had
brought. That night I couldn't sleep, it hurt so bad, and the
next morning when the Sergeant told us to finish work in
the field because the sun was shining again, I said my foot
hurt and maybe I should stay off it for a day.

The Sergeant said it would be better for me to walk on it
so it wouldn't get stiff. I took a burlap bag and wrapped my
bandaged foot in it, because I couldn't get my boot on, and
I went to work harrowing. It didn't hurt much, as I was
walking all day behind the horses, but when I got back to
the house and took the burlap off I noticed it was bleeding
again. I couldn't get the bandage off, it was stuck to my
foot. Kristina came over again with hot water and a clean
bandage. When I got the bandage off, I could see that the
swelling was worse and my foot was all red. The next day
was Sabbath and I stayed off my foot all day, soaking it
most of the time.

Sunday I refused to go to work and my boss finally came
over to look at my foot. He said I could stay home and keep
soaking it. I told him I thought I should see a doctor, but
his answer was: Where would I get you a doctor! I said he
could let me take a wagon to town and I could see our fam-

ily doctor there. He said I should wait until Tuesday and he would take me to the army doctor, and in the meantime I didn't have to work and could stay in my room. For the next two days, I stayed in bed most of the time. My foot hurt a lot and I had chills and felt sick all over my body. I didn't want to eat anything, but Kristina made me vegetable soup.

She was very good to me and treated me like one of her children. I told her that when I went home this time I wasn't going to come back. She said she was sorry to hear that and that she would miss me. She had tears in her eyes when she told me to sleep well and she would see me in the morning. I asked her not to say anything to the Sergeant about my not coming back. My buddies and I talked it over and they decided not to come back either. I told them to pack their clothes and take them along as though they were going to have them washed, and not to tell the Sergeant they weren't coming back.

Tuesday morning we harnessed the horses and waited for the Sergeant. My foot was very bad, I couldn't even walk on it. When the boss came to the wagon he wanted to know why we were taking all our belongings with us. We said we were taking them home to be washed and to bring back warmer clothes for the winter. That seemed to satisfy him. We started out for the city and got there about eleven-thirty . . .

As the Sergeant drove off in the wagon to get supplies, the boys headed inside for their pay, Lazar with his arm over Boris's shoulder for support and holding his boot in the other hand. They nearly collided with Rittmeister Konreid who was on his way out. He recognized Lazar and, seeing his bandaged foot, asked what had happened.

They all stood on the porch as Lazar told the Rittmeister

the story about the accident with the ax and about the Sergeant making him continue to work and refusing to let him come to town to see a doctor until today. The Rittmeister kept shaking his head. When Lazar finished, the Rittmeister motioned them inside and he called out for his Sergeant Major.

"Feldwebel Schultz!"

The Feldwebel came out of his office and joined the group.

"Jawohl, Herr Rittmeister?"

"Lassen sie den Jungen sofort ins Lazarett bringen. Ein Doktor soll seinen Fuss untersuchen," he said, issuing instructions for the foot to be examined immediately, "und mir einen Befund senden. Befehlen Sie, Feldwebel Müller, sich sofort bei mir zu melden!" He was also ordering that Sergeant Müller report to him at once.

"Jawohl, Herr Rittmeister!"

The Feldwebel went off to make the arrangements and Rittmeister Konreid went back into his office to await Sergeant Müller. Lazar was given a chair outside his office and told to wait. Meanwhile, the boys had gotten their pay and Lazar's, and when they returned to give him his money, he asked them to stop at his house on their way home to let his parents know what was going on and to tell them not to worry, that he would be home after he saw the doctor at the field hospital. The boys left and Lazar sat waiting.

In a few minutes, Hermann came in, frowning and out of breath. He knocked on the Rittmeister's door, glancing down at Lazar in the chair, but saying nothing. Seeing Lazar, he now knew what this was all about.

"Herein!" commanded the Rittmeister from inside. Hermann went into the office, shutting the door behind him. Lazar only heard snatches of the conversation, but it was obvious from what he heard that Hermann was being severely reprimanded.

110

"... diese Leute sind keine Sklaven! ... branchen ihre Mitarbeit! ... Sie sind ein Feldwebel des Kaisers Armee! ... unmöglich ... sollten den Jungen früher behandelt haben lassen! ... froh sein, dass kein Wundfieber eingesetzt hat!"

Wundfieber? Lazar had heard that word before. *Lucky if he didn't have Wundfieber? Gangrene! The Rittmeister was saying they would be lucky if Lazar didn't have gangrene! He wasn't quite sure what that meant, but it didn't sound good and that worried him. The Rittmeister was still yelling at Hermann.*

"Ist das klar, Feldwebel? Ist das klar!"

"Jawohl, Herr Rittmeister!"

For some reason, Hermann's dressing down was bringing Lazar no satisfaction. In fact it made him uncomfortable. It wasn't that he liked the Sergeant, but after spending most of the summer with him on the farm, especially after seeing the picture of his family with its inscription, Lazar had come to know Hermann as a person and as one of his group. It was one thing for Lazar and his two friends to curse Hermann among themselves, but it was another somehow to hear someone outside the group bawl him out for the same thing.

Lazar was doubly relieved therefore to see his old friend Gustav who had come to take him to the doctor. He didn't want to have to face Hermann when he came out of the office. Gustav helped Lazar into a wagon and drove him to the field hospital at the rebuilt army post on the south end of town. On the way they caught up with each other's summer. When Gustav heard about Lazar's life on the farm, he told Lazar that if he wanted to work again after his foot was healed, it might be possible for him to get Lazar assigned to the stable. That sounded good to Lazar, because he had definitely decided not to return to the farm.

ᛯ

When they arrived at the field hospital, a doctor was waiting to examine Lazar's foot. He sat in a chair as the doctor used a scissors to cut off the bandage and for the first time since the accident, Lazar was frightened. The Rittmeister's words to Hermann hadn't helped. The foot was swollen and red and the area around the wound was white. The doctor pressed gently around the wound with his thumb and a small amount of pus oozed from it. Lazar yelled out in pain and instinctively pulled his foot back.

The doctor looked at Gustav. "It's a good thing you got him in here. Another day or two and he would have been in real trouble. I'll have to lance it." He turned to Lazar. "Now, boy, this is going to hurt. I have to open this up so the pus will drain. Hold onto your friend here and look out the window, and it will be over in just a minute, all right?"

Lazar nodded through his tears. He squeezed Gustav's hand with both of his and looked away. He wanted to be brave, but when the doctor cut his foot it hurt like hell and he couldn't help screaming. Ow! Ow! Ow! He was still screaming when he heard the doctor telling him it was all over. He felt dizzy and sick to his stomach. The doctor handed Gustav a bottle of smelling salts to hold under Lazar's nose as he bandaged the foot, and by time that was done Lazar was feeling better.

The doctor wrote out a brief report for Gustav to take back to the Rittmeister, meanwhile telling Lazar to soak the foot three times a day in hot water, the rest of the time to sit or lie down with the foot elevated on a pillow, and to come back in three days. Then Gustav drove him home. The Rittmeister's instructions had been for Lazar to stay home until his foot healed. If he chose to return to work after that, he would be paid for his sick leave at his regular wages.

Gustav saw to it that Lazar was settled in his house, had a glass of tea with Lazar's parents, and left to return to work. For the next hour or two, Lazar sat on the leather sofa in the living room with his foot on a big pillow and told his parents and Frumke all about the last five weeks, his work, the accident, his trip to the doctor, the Rittmeister's concern. Finally, the excitement and tensions of the past few days caught up with Lazar. Exhausted, he fell asleep on the sofa.

Dinnertime came and they let him sleep. He woke up briefly during the night and found his mother sitting near him in a chair, waiting to feed him. He ate some cold chicken, cake and milk, and then went back to sleep, this time in his own bed with Rosetka curled up at his side like the old days. It was good to be home.

Chapter Six

1. ↲

[Spring 1916. It had been a quiet winter. His foot finally healed, Lazar had gone to work in the fall helping Gustav in the stable. Later he had been transferred to light duty in the warehouse under the Feldwebel. It was a soft job, his first since going to work for the Germans, and Lazar had been able to spend the winter at home with his family. His father now spent almost all of his time in bed. With Lazar's pay of two and a half Marks, the rent, and the milk products from Belka which they were able to sell, the family was still managing. News of the war was sporadic, but the Germans were not doing well at the Front. So far it had had little effect on the routine of occupied ˎVolkovysk.

In April Lazar was called into the Feldwebel's office. The Germans had decided to grow a large vegetable garden on several acres of land adjacent to the army post. Lazar was offered the job of supervising the garden at an increase in wages to four Marks a day. It meant that he would have to live in a small two-room furnished brick house next to the field, but he would not be required to work on the Sabbath and would be within easy walking distance of his home. He would also have all the help he

114

*would need and would have authorization to draw from
prison labor and to hire peasants whenever he needed.*

*Lazar was excited by the offer and accepted. By the end
of April he was settled into the brick house. The field had
been cleaned and burned, spread with manure, and was
now ready for plowing.*]

It was the first Sunday in May. I went to the village and
spoke to the head man. I told him that I was in need of five
plows, horses and men to start Monday at eight plowing
the field. He assured me that I would get what I wanted. It
took three days and the plowing was done. I had an order
from Herr Rittmeister's office to get Russian prisoners, as
many as I needed and whenever I needed them. Since it
was very close, I could walk over in the afternoon and
make arrangements for the next day. The field had to be
raked and beds made ready for planting. I had all the tools
I needed.

The weather was just perfect. It was warmer and there
was no longer a danger of frost, so I made arrangements
for several women from the village, and between them
and the Russian prisoners I had my planting done by the
middle of May. I also planted about three acres of potatoes.
For the next couple of weeks there was little to do but wait
for rain and watch the garden grow. I was able to walk
home almost every night.

Summer came and it got warm and the sun was shining
every day, and the garden grew by leaps and bounds. But
so did the weeds. I had to get girls every day to weed the
garden. They were all teenagers from fifteen to eighteen
years old and they were full of fun; singing and laughing
and joking, especially at lunchtime. They all would sit under a big tree and I would be with them. They liked me
and decided to have fun with me . . .

❦

The game had been going on all week and each day it went a little further. They would all sit in a circle under the big tree, Lazar and the girls, and they would eat their lunch. Lazar always sat next to Natalia, the pretty dark-haired girl with flashing eyes and a quick smile. While the other girls gossiped and joked, mostly about the boys in their village, Natalia was always teasing Lazar about being too serious, and occasionally she would reach over and tickle him to get him to smile. Lazar liked Natalia the best. She was sixteen and full of mischief. It was she who had instigated the game on Monday.

Lazar would finish his lunch, feign a yawn, stretch, lie back and pretend to take a nap. On Monday he had actually been sleepy and intended to nap. Now, of course, he could hardly wait to finish lunch so the game could begin. Sleep was out of the question. After a minute or two the girls' conversation would change to whispers and giggles, shushing each other not to wake Lazar from his "nap."

Then Natalia would slowly unbutton his shirt, at the same time blowing softly in his ear, her hair falling gently on his face (how he loved it!), and suddenly dozens of fingertips would be running up and down his chest and stomach, while others crept lightly up his calves beneath his pants legs. Now and then he would sneak an eye open and there would always be a girl standing over his head, legs apart, hands on her hips, posing, and Lazar would look straight up her dress. None of the girls wore anything underneath their dresses.

By this time the girls would have noticed the bulge in Lazar's pants and would be unable to contain their giggling. Lazar, reaching the limit of his endurance at the hands of these exquisite torturers, would stretch and yawn and pretend to be awakening, the cue for the girls to race back to their spot in the circle and sit down while Natalia finished buttoning Lazar's shirt. Then Lazar would open his eyes, sit up, comment that he must have dozed off and announce that it was time to get back to work. Everyone would pretend that absolutely nothing had happened. Except, of course, that for the rest of the afternoon Lazar would walk around with cramps and for the last two nights he had even had a wet dream. Still, it was a great game and, cramps or no cramps, he was looking forward to playing it again today!

They sat down to lunch in a circle as they always did, no, not exactly as they always did, something was different this time. Each of the girls had their legs apart today, knees slightly raised so their dresses slid well up on their thighs, and as usual they had no pants on. Another thing, instead of tickling him as she had been doing all week, Natalia twice reached over and squeezed his inner thigh in full view of the others, whose jokes about the village boys were becoming more graphic than ever. Lazar sensed that the game was being played differently today, but he knew only what he had learned earlier in the week, so, despite the already obvious bulge under his pants, he proceeded to yawn, lie back and pretend to nap.

As soon as his eyes closed, the girls were up and Natalia unbuttoned his shirt, this time flicking her tongue in and out of his ear. One of the girls whispered to Natalia: "Slabo tebe rasstegnut shtany I dostat' do pipki da vyudit' rybku!"—I dare you to unbutton his pants and jerk him off!

Natalia laughed, yanked at the remaining buttons on his shirt and shifted her attention to his pants. Lazar didn't know what to do, so he just kept his eyes shut and waited. Hands now held him gently at the wrists and ankles as his pants were unbuttoned and peeled to his knees. Squeals of delight greeted his now exposed and throbbing erection. It seemed like hundreds of dancing fingers were tickling him all over his chest, stomach, thighs, balls, everywhere at once, and a hand, Natalia's, wrapped warmly around his cock and began to move up and down, up and down faster and faster and Lazar couldn't help himself his body began to move down and up in time with Natalia's hand moving up and down faster faster and he felt it begin like an itch being scratched deep down inside coming coming he couldn't hold it back now as it came rising up up and up and out in heaving pulsing warmth that swept over him with a feeling he had never before experienced!

A cheer went up from the girls as Lazar's semen erupted, shooting straight up in the air and falling onto his stomach in a cascade of warm viscosity, cooling almost instantly and running down his sides as he rolled over onto his stomach and tugged frantically at his pants. There was no gradual "awakening" this time, no point in further pretense. Lazar was terribly embarrassed. The girls, realizing that perhaps they had gone too far with their game, needed no prompting to get back to work. By the time he stood up, they were already back at their weeding, working feverishly, their grinning faces turned away from where Lazar now stood buttoning his shirt, his eyes filled with tears.

... I felt ashamed. The next week I stopped having lunch with them and I concentrated on managing the garden. The girls realized that I was angry about the whole thing and told me how sorry they were for what they had done to me. I told them to forget it. They said, *"Prostite nas, pozhaluista. Davaite otobedaem vmeste vznak togo, chto vy ne serdites'. Nam, pravda ochen' zhal', chto tak poluchilos',"* which meant they were sorry and wanted me to have lunch with them so they would know I wasn't angry. They promised not to fool around with me. I said,

"Ladno, no tol'ko chtob bol'she bez fokusov" . . . all right, but no more funny stuff.

So I sat with them at lunch and told them all was forgotten. But I confess that I didn't dislike what they had done to me, I found it very exciting. By that Friday all the weeding was done. I told the girls I would contact them the next time I needed them. I was glad that week was over. Except for going to synagogue early in the morning, I slept most of the day Saturday. Late in the afternoon, I took a walk with Frumke and I told her about what the girls did to me. Frumke had a good laugh.

2. ✢

It was the middle of June. I had an idea to rent an orchard from the Germans. My father thought it was a good idea, that it would give him a chance to get out of the house too, and my mother agreed. The next day the Feldwebel and the Rittmeister visited me at the garden. The garden looked beautiful and a lot of the early vegetables were ready to be picked. The Feldwebel told me to pick whatever I thought was ready and he would send a wagon with baskets the next day.

Meanwhile, Herr Rittmeister walked around the garden talking to the German guards. Then he came back and told me that I had done a very good job. I stood at attention while he talked and when he finished, I thanked him and asked if I could see him in his office during the week. He told me to talk to the Feldwebel about an appointment. I arranged to come the next afternoon after the vegetables were picked.

The next day I picked several baskets of vegetables and then rode to headquarters in the wagon. I reported to the

Rittmeister and stood at attention just like a soldier. He smiled. I knew that he liked me to do that. He said, "I want to compliment you on the good job you did. You made a fine garden out of an empty field. Now, what can I do for you?" I told him about my father being sick and confined to bed most of the time, and that I am the only one able to work to help my parents with the little money that I am earning. I told him that before my father was sick he had been in the fruit business and that maybe it would do him some good to be around an orchard again, so would it be possible to rent one of their orchards near town?

Herr Rittmeister said, "I'll do better than that, I'll let you have one of our orchards for the summer and all you have to do is give the soldiers on the farm enough fruit for them, the rest is yours." Then he asked if that meant I would no longer be able to work for them. I said oh no, I would continue to work until the garden was finished in the middle of September and then I would go help harvest the fruit. He said *"Das ist gut!"* and he called the Feldwebel in and told him about our talk and that he is to write a letter to the farm nearest the city ordering the sergeant in charge to give us his cooperation.

I had tears in my eyes when I thanked the Rittmeister and I went home to tell my parents all about it. Mother was so happy that she took me in her arms and hugged me and kissed me. My father was very pleased. That Sunday I hired a wagon and we drove out to see the orchard about twenty kilometers from town. There were about 100 trees, mostly apples and pears and plums. The sergeant in charge was not too pleased to get the orders, but there was nothing he could do about it. He wanted to know who is going to take care of the orchard and I told him that we would hire a man from the village as a watchman and that my parents would be there too. I also told him about how I had been working for the Germans ever since they took over our city, and by time we left, the sergeant was in a much better mood.

We went to the village and we were able to hire an old man to be our watchman for three months starting in July. On the way home I noticed quite a change in my father's frame of mind, he seemed happy. I went back to work the next day. The garden was coming along beautifully and was loaded with cucumbers, beets, carrots, lettuce and cabbage, tomatoes and squash. Most of my workers were now Russian prisoners and they were not fed very well. I told them they could help themselves to all the vegetables they could eat while they were at the garden, and they did.

However, they took advantage of that and began to steal vegetables for their comrades back in camp and it was getting out of hand. I told them not to do it anymore and they promised they wouldn't, but a few days later I noticed they had their shirts full of cucumbers and other vegetables. I stopped them as they were leaving the field and I told the guards. The guards started to hit them across their backs and ordered them to empty out their shirts and never to do that again. I really felt bad about the beating they got, but they wouldn't listen to me and I had no choice.

The next day they told me they were sorry and that they didn't blame me for reporting it to the guards. They promised they wouldn't do it again and I told them it was all right to continue to eat as much as they wanted while they worked. We started to work in the potato patch, so I told them they could build a fire and roast potatoes for themselves for lunch. They thanked me and said that I was very kind.

It was the middle of July. The watchman had moved to the orchard on the first and had built a hut according to our agreement. Belka was farmed out at our Polish neighbor's and my parents and Frumke left for the orchard. I told them I would come for weekends. On Fridays my replacement would come to the garden, I would give him instructions on what to do, and then I would walk all the way to the orchard, getting there by nightfall. Sometimes I got a ride with a passing wagon, but most of the time I had to walk. I used to get so scared walking through the woods that I would run as fast as I could to get past them. My father would get angry with me for walking that late on the Sabbath. I never argued with him because I didn't want him to get sick.

I didn't like the idea of my parents having to sleep in a hut, so I arranged with the sergeant for them to use a little house near the big farmhouse which he and two other soldiers occupied. The little house was empty and there was no glass in the windows. I closed in the windows with bricks and I built a platform for them to sleep on. We cleaned out the room and fixed it up as best we could. Cooking had to be done outside and on rainy days Mother couldn't cook at all. Every two weeks she hired a wagon to take her to the city for their food. I was getting a good idea what my parents had put up with all their lives, taking care of orchards.

The garden produced a bumper crop. Every day I sent a wagon full of vegetables to the main warehouse. By the middle of September the garden was harvested. With the help of the Russian prisoners I cleaned out the field in a few days so that it would be ready for plowing in the spring. The weather was getting cold. I reported to the Feldwebel at the end of the week and told him that there was no more work in the garden. He wanted to know if I wanted to go back to work for him in the warehouse and I told him that I would like a month's leave of absence so I could help my parents with the orchard. He told me to wait and he would get permission from the Rittmeister.

In a few minutes they both came out. I stood at attention. Herr Rittmeister told me to relax. He told me that he had enjoyed my vegetables all summer and that I had done an excellent job. Then he told me he had instructed the Feldwebel to give me my leave of absence and to pay me for that month as a bonus. I couldn't believe my ears! I thanked Herr Rittmeister and told him how much I appreciated his kindness. He told me that I could come back to work after the fruit was picked and that if I needed anything or had any problems, I should get in touch with the Feldwebel. Then he said *Wiedersehen!* and went back inside.

It was the end of the second week that I had spent with my parents at the orchard. Mother had already taken three wagonloads of early fruit to market and had it sold in one day. Now we were waiting for the winter apples and pears to be full grown. On Friday morning the old watchman requested Saturday and Saturday night off, but he promised to send his son for Saturday night so that we would not be left alone to guard the orchard. We thought nothing of it and said of course it was all right, especially because his son who was twenty-seven would take his place.

Saturday night the watchman's son came. We ate supper with my parents and then I told them to go to their room and that the watchman's son and I would stand guard all night. It was a very dark night and we kept walking around the orchard. It was about midnight when we sat down to rest. It was windy and dark and the wind was whistling through the trees. There were dogs barking and you could hear fruit dropping from the trees and to top it off, the watchman's son started telling me ghost stories and it got me scared.

It must have been about one in the morning when I suddenly saw someone strike a match about twenty-five yards away from us at a section where the best fruit was. I asked the watchman's son if he had seen that and he said no, he hadn't seen anything. Then another match was struck and I knew someone was there. I said let's go and I started to walk toward the spot where I had seen the match. The watchman's son was behind me. I saw someone start to run with a bag of fruit. I yelled and started to run after him. When he got to the fence he couldn't make it over with the bag of fruit and he had to drop it. Then I realized that it was our own watchman, the old man.

I grabbed him by his coat and screamed for help. His son stayed back and wouldn't help me. I held onto his coat but he got to the other side of the fence, and then he struck me on my forehead with a small hatchet that he had in his hand. Lucky for me it was not the sharp side of the hatchet. I was still holding onto his coat, so he slipped out of his coat and ran away. By that time my parents heard me and came running.

My father got upset and started yelling at the watchman's son for not helping me. The son claimed he didn't know his father was planning to rob the orchard. By now the sergeant came to find out what the yelling was about, but he didn't stay long and soon went back to the house saying to call him if we needed him. I had a big lump on my forehead from where the watchman had hit me and I was still scared, so my parents stayed up the rest of the night with me.

In the morning we got the bag of apples and we found the old man's hatchet and sheepskin coat. The old man never showed up again, not even for his pay. He disappeared from the village and no one knew where he had gone. We hired a replacement to stay until the fruit was picked.

ᚦ

It was a week before the High Holidays and it was time for my parents to go home. We picked three wagonloads of the big black plums and two loads of apples and then they left. Frumke and I stayed on with the new watchman. We hired boys and girls from the village and picked apples and pears. Two days before Yom Kippur I sent Frumke home with a wagon full of fruit. On the last day I loaded everything that was left and headed home, but by the time everything was unloaded it was past sundown and I got home too late to eat before the fast started.

In the middle of the next day I was in synagogue praying and I was so hungry and tired that I passed out. Mother took me home but Father wouldn't let me eat until sundown. Frumke went to the Rabbi and asked him what to do, and he said to let me have a spoonful of milk every hour until sundown. That was a summer and fall that I will never forget the rest of my life.

Chapter Seven

1. ⮤

On the sixth of April 1917 the United States declared war on Germany. There was a lot of activity in our city. The trains were busy once again with troops traveling to the Front. Our city was left with only a small force as all the younger men were shipped out. The Germans began to fall back on all their lines and once again Volkovysk was in the middle of it all.

There were rumors that the Germans would burn everything to the ground when they retreat and that they would take livestock with them, but we had heard these rumors before about the Russians and nothing had happened, so we didn't pay too much attention to them. The weather was getting warmer and the farmers took to the fields. Many of the Russians who had left their farms before the Germans came were now returning, but most of them had no livestock and they needed horses especially, so they could work their fields. A booming business opened up smuggling horses through the German lines from Russia.

One night a cousin of my mother's came to the house and asked me if I would like to help him bring back horses that he would buy in a market about fifty kilometers away.

He explained that we would have to ride them at night, because that was the safest time. The Germans never patrolled the roads at night. He said he would share his profits and I would have a good chance to make some money. I agreed, but my parents were against it and told me not to. After a lot of discussion, they finally agreed.

The next morning my cousin and I walked to the nearest point of the highway and picked up a ride with one of the wagons that was traveling to the market. By nighttime we were there. We stayed in an inn overnight and the next morning we went out to buy the horses. They were being hidden from the police. We bought six horses and when it got dark we started for home. We had to ride fast if we were to get there by daybreak. We each took three horses abreast, riding the one in the middle bareback. We got home at dawn and put them in my stable.

I watered them and fed them and went to sleep. When I got up later in the day I could hardly stand up. Riding bareback for ten hours is no easy job. There were a lot of horse dealers from Bialystok in town and they were buying any horse they could find. We had our horses sold the same day. The poor horses had very little rest and they were off again. We made a good profit. The next day we took off again and we stayed in the same inn overnight. In the morning my cousin was gone before I got up and, not knowing where he had gone, I decided to go to the open market to see if there were any horses for sale. The police didn't seem to bother anybody when it was only one horse for sale here or there.

I saw one horse that I liked and since the price was low and I couldn't find my cousin to ask his advice, I bought it. When my cousin finally got back, I showed him my bargain. He let out a yell: Oh no! and I asked what was wrong and he said, "Didn't you see this horse is swaybacked? You won't be able to get rid of him!" I said so what, I'll keep him for myself, but on the way home after dark he yelled to me that he would try to sell my horse along with his. His horses were beautiful, so whoever wanted his bad enough would have to take mine with them. As it turned out, that's what happened and I made a few rubles profit on my horse.

We continued this operation for several weeks and I made a few hundred rubles, but I didn't want to continue smuggling horses anymore. I decided that I would buy one good horse and travel to Bialystok, buying herring, flour and sugar, and other goods, and selling them to our stores in Volkovysk. My cousin said that would be dangerous and that if I got caught by the police they would take the horse and wagon, but I said what we had been doing was just as dangerous, so I was willing to take the risk. On our next trip I bought a very beautiful black mare, about six years old and very fast. I assembled my wagon and harness and I was ready to start traveling to Bialystok.

Actually, I got the idea from Chatzkol, a friend of mine who was much older than me and had already made several trips to Bialystok. Chatzkol was about five feet six inches tall and very skinny. His family had a store where they sold all kinds of milk goods and we knew them well. My mother went to see him and got him to promise that he would look after me. He told her not to worry, he would travel with me and see that I was all right.

Word went out that I would be traveling to the big city and before I knew it, I had five merchants for passengers, and so did Chatzkol. We started out about four o'clock in the afternoon, making several stops to feed and rest the horses. The trip took between twenty-four and thirty hours from Volkovysk to Bialystok, but the merchants didn't have much choice as the railroad was once again being used exclusively for military purposes. We arrived the next night and stayed at an inn where all the wagons stayed and where merchants came to hire wagons to take their merchandise to their cities. I made up my mind to buy whatever I could and be in business for myself.

The next day Chatzkol and I went to the wholesale places and bought six barrels of herring, three for each of us. We started out after dark so that we would not be noticed by the police. It was against the law to transport goods from one city to another without paying duty and the duty was too high to make it pay, so what we were doing was considered smuggling. However, once out of the city and on the road, we were relatively safe at night. We had no trouble getting rid of the herring when we got back.

I made these trips weekly, but I never knew what day I would leave Volkovysk, it depended on when I would fill up with passengers. Sometimes I would even have to stay over on the Sabbath. One week Chatzkol had a load of rabbit skins that was too big for one wagon and he asked if I would use my wagon too and between us we could deliver the rabbit skins to Bialystok. I said yes. We loaded up and started out. On the way, to keep awake, we rode in each other's wagon and talked.

Chatzkol started to ask me about my love life, whether I had a girl friend and if I had gotten laid. I told him no, I didn't, and he said, "I'll have to do something about that. After all, if you're going to work like a man, you should live like one." He told me that he must have a lay at least once or twice a week. I asked him with whom and he said at the bardak on my street, and the next time he goes there he will take me and see to it that I get laid.

I didn't say yes or no. I said, "You're twenty-six years old. Why don't you get married? Then you wouldn't have to go to a bardak."

He said, "With a wife, it's the same all the time. At a bardak I have a different one every time."

A few days after we got back from the trip, Chatzkol

came over to take me with him to the bardak. I told him in no way was I going to commit a sinful act like that. Well, he gave up on me and from that time on he never talked to me about it again. In fact, he got very angry with me because I didn't want to go with him.

The weekend passed and I didn't hear from him, so I went over to his father's store and found out that he had taken a few passengers who were in a big hurry to get to Bialystok. His father also told me that he heard there were a lot of things available in the Bialystok warehouses, so I decided to make a trip and see what I could buy. I went to the fur factory and they had a load of wet rabbit skins for me to take to Bialystok. I loaded up and started out . . .

It was late afternoon by the time they finished loading the wagon with the bundles of wet rabbit skins and Lazar finally headed for Bialystok. He had been hoping for an earlier start, but now the sun was almost down and it was turning cold. It was going to be a long cold night before he reached the inn at the halfway mark. Good thing he'd brought the extra blanket.

Good thing too that he had managed to bring in all that wood for the house the last two days, not that he hadn't been scared half to death in the process. The Germans had been using Russian prisoners to cut wood in the forest on the north side of town and Lazar had discovered that there were no guards posted on the woodpile at night. In the last two nights Lazar had made four trips to the woodpile and had taken enough wood home to last them the whole winter.

But it had been a frightening experience, not so much because of the risk of being caught by the Germans—after all, he was not without friends at headquarters, and if he was caught he was certain he would be able to talk his way out of it—there was little enough money to live on these days, let alone to buy wood with, and free wood was well worth that risk. No, what frightened Lazar most was the thought of wild animals and escaped Russian prisoners roaming the forest at night. There had been stories of people getting beaten and robbed by half-starved escapees, and each time Lazar made a trip to the forest at night, he was fearful of attack by wolves or escaped prisoners. There were many ominous sounds in the forest at night.

Lazar shivered, partly from the recollection of his trips to the woodpile at night and partly from the cold which was getting worse. To keep warm and to stay awake, he periodically got down from the wagon, as he did now, and ran alongside his horse holding the harness with one hand, pretending that he too was a horse and that he and the mare were both pulling the wagon, their gait synchronized in a brisk trot, their warm breath escaping to the chill night air in long vaporized puffs of white. Occasionally, he even tossed his head and snorted the way the mare sometimes did when she was feeling particularly good, and when he did that she would look over at him out of the corner of her eye and snort back, as if to remind him that she was real and he was only a fake horse, and he laughed.

Pretending to be a horse warmed him and kept him awake; it also helped to pass the time. This was his first trip to Bialystok alone and it seemed much longer without Chatzkol to talk to, especially at night. Tiring finally and out of breath, Lazar slowed the mare to a walk and climbed back into the wagon. They were approaching a stretch of the road that ran through a thick forest and Lazar felt a bit more secure sitting high up in the wagon than down on the road with his horse.

131

He began to talk to the mare, it calmed him to do so, and the mare pointed one of her ears back toward him while the other remained erect and intent on monitoring the sounds on the road ahead.

"Now don't you worry, horse, there's nothing for you to worry about as long as you have me at the reins. We've been through these woods before with Chatzkol, remember? and nothing ever happened to us, right? So just keep going, we have a long way to go yet. Move along, hurry up! When we get to the inn in the morning, I'll buy you some nice oats and ... hey, what's wrong?"

The mare had shifted both ears to the front and instead of speeding up, slowed down, as though she heard or sensed something in the darkness ahead.

"What do you hear, horse? Do you hear something or are you just trying to scare me? Come on now, move along, faster! There's nothing out there I tell you."

But there was something out there, the mare sensed it, and now Lazar sensed it too and he was frightened. What was it? Suddenly, the mare stopped altogether and stood rigidly still, her flanks quivering, her nostrils flared, her eyes wide with fear and looking straight out into the darkness. Lazar strained but he could see nothing, hear nothing. He snapped the reins several times and clucked softly, but the mare wouldn't move. Something ahead had frightened her and whatever it was, she now debated whether to wait it out or bolt. Waiting for her to decide, Lazar gathered in the reins to be ready. His teeth were chattering and his hands had begun to shake. What was it out there? Or who?

Then he saw them. They came out of the woods on the right and crossed the road in single file to the other side, not more than twenty-five meters in front of the wagon. Wolves! Oh god, wolves! Lazar held his breath. What should he do? Wolves are supposed to be afraid of fire.

*There was straw in the wagon, but he had no matches!
What if the mare whinnied or stamped her foot? They
would hear her and come after them!*

*But the mare stood quietly, shivering but not making a
sound. There were at least ten or twelve of them, big gray
ones, their winter coats glistening brightly in the black
night, and Lazar and the mare watched as one by one they
crossed the road and disappeared into the woods. Was it
possible that they could pass so close and not see them?
Then Lazar realized that the wind was blowing away from
the wolves and not toward them. It seemed like they were
not going to be discovered by the wolves. Once, the last in
line paused briefly in the middle of the road and sniffed
the air, and Lazar held his breath, waiting, but then the
wolf discovered that it was being left behind and it broke
into an easy lope to catch up with the pack.*

*The road was empty again. Lazar prayed the mare
wouldn't take it into her head to bolt now, before the
wolves were safely out of range. He needn't have worried.
The mare's instinct for preservation was stronger than her
fear and she too waited. Then, deciding that it was safe at
last and not waiting for Lazar's command, the mare broke
into a wild gallop as if the Devil himself were in hot pur-
suit, and it took Lazar a good ten minutes to get her back
under control, slowing her first to a canter, then to a trot,
and finally to a fast walk.*

*In a way, getting the runaway horse under control was a
big help in settling Lazar down too, and by the time he
managed to get the mare slowed to a walk he was no
longer frightened. In fact he wasn't even cold, just sleepy.
Very sleepy. As the horse settled back into her regular
pace, Lazar pulled the blanket up around his shoulders,
slouched down in the corner of the seat and fell fast asleep.*

ꝑ

It might have been five minutes or it might have been two hours, there was no way to tell. Lazar slept soundly and dreamed. He dreamed of Natalia and the girls, lying back on the warm ground under the big tree, the girls giggling and caressing him. Then they picked him up by his hands and feet and began to swing his body back and forth. One! Two! Three! and they threw him high in the air, he soared higher and higher, higher than the big tree, and he looked back at them and laughed and laughed.

But then he began to fall and it was no longer fun! Falling, falling, faster and faster, and he became terribly frightened! He tumbled head over heels through the air and he yelled out: Help! When he finally hit the ground, it was hard and cold and he awoke with a start to find himself lying in the field next to the road, the wagon on its side, wheels still spinning, and the mare down too, wheezing and choking in her harness, her legs flailing wildly in the air!

Dazed, Lazar stumbled over to the mare and grabbed at the twisted harness, finally working it loose and off. Freed, she scrambled to her feet unhurt, shook herself twice and then, as though nothing at all had happened, she ambled away to graze on the grass. Lazar leaned on the wagon for support and looked around. It was growing light. He couldn't understand how the wagon had overturned, but here it was, on its side in the field, rabbit skins strewn all over the road.

He limped to the road, his left leg must have been hurt in the fall, and began to gather up the skins, doing his best to rebundle them. It was a frustrating task. The skins had frozen during the night and were like stiff boards, no longer fitting into the same neat bundles. When he finished, the pile on the side of the road was so big he was afraid they might not all fit into the wagon. Next, he tried to right the wagon, first by pulling it and, when that didn't work, by pushing it, but it was no use. He thought of using a pole to wedge it up. There was nothing but open fields as far as he could see, nothing to use for a pole. He would have to wait for help to come along.

The sun was up and there would be wagons coming soon from the other direction, because he knew approximately where he was now and realized that he was only about an hour from the inn. Sure enough, in a short while a wagon came into view with two men driving a load of herring barrels to Slonim. They stopped to help Lazar and in a matter of minutes the wagon was right side up again and back on the road. Lazar thanked the men, waved good-bye, and proceeded to reload the wagon. The frozen skins were piled precariously high, but they would be all right if Lazar was careful until the sun thawed them out. He hitched up the mare and drove the rest of the way to the inn, where he stayed long enough to eat and feed the horse before continuing on to Bialystok.

. . . I got to Bialystok about midnight and the next day I delivered the skins. I was glad to get them out of the wagon. Then I went to the wholesale houses. They were empty. Nothing to buy and no buyers either, so I was unable to pick up any passengers to go back home with me. I started for home alone with an empty wagon. I had lost almost a day due to my mishap.

The second night I was about fifty kilometers from home. It was another freezing night. In order to keep warm I ran alongside my horse for a while. Then I got back up on my wagon. My horse knew the way home. I fell asleep again, not even knowing that I was falling asleep . . .

ᚦ

The last thing Lazar said to his horse before he fell asleep was that she should stay awake. Often on these long trips the mare would pull the wagon in her sleep, which is probably what had happened on the way to Bialystok with the rabbit skins. With the mare and Lazar both asleep that night, the mare must have walked too close to the side of the road, putting two wheels over the embankment and finally turning the wagon over and herself with it. Lazar was not anxious for that to happen again, so he was very clear to the mare: Stay awake, horse! Then he fell asleep.

In his dream Lazar was sleeping. He dreamed that someone was shaking him by the shoulder and trying to wake him up. In his dream he didn't want to wake up, he wanted to continue sleeping. Now the person in his dream was shaking him harder and shouting for him to wake up. He tried to turn away and not to listen, but it was hopeless, there was just no way to sleep through this racket, and in his dream Lazar finally was forced to wake up.

Only it was no dream! Lazar's eyes banged open to find four strange men in his wagon staring at him, one of them was still shaking him roughly by the shoulder and shouting at him to wake up! Wide awake and badly frightened, Lazar stared back at the men. Escaped prisoners. They looked exactly like the ones that were always being recaptured and paraded through Volkovysk on their way back to camp. Fierce-looking men with wild beards, their heads wrapped with wide strips of torn blanket tied under the chin, their bodies appearing grotesque in the many layers of clothing they had managed to scavenge in order to keep warm, and smelling stale and sour from not having bathed in weeks or even months.

But mostly it was their eyes that scared Lazar, it was the eyes that reflected the anguish and desperation of half-starved fugitives who wanted only to make it home to their families, to be warm and clean and not hungry anymore, instead of scavenging like rats.

"A ty patsan, kuda?" (Hey kid, where're ya goin'?)

Lazar tried to answer, but nothing seemed to come out. His teeth chattered instead and he began to shiver. The man, realizing that he was frightening the boy, softened his voice.

"Ne boisia. Ne obidim." (Don't be afraid. We won't hurt you.) "A ty patsan?"

Reassured more by the new tone in the man's voice than by his words, which Lazar only half caught anyway, his heart was pounding that loudly in his ears, he cleared his throat and managed a stammering one-word response.

"Vol ... Volkovysk."

Impatient, one of the other men growled, "U tebia est' chto poest'?" (Do you have anything to eat?) The first man then repeated the question in a soft but demanding voice.

"U nas est' nemnogo khleba i dva iabloka," Lazar answered politely. (We have some bread and two apples.) He reached to the bag at his feet and passed the food to the man nearest him. The man tore off a big bite of bread with his teeth and passed the bread to the others who did the same, meanwhile producing a wicked-looking knife which he used to cut the two apples into halves. He gave each man a half and for the next few minutes the four men ate the apple, core and all, and finished off the bread.

Lazar was rapidly calming down. Watching four grown and obviously hungry men make a meal of two apples and half a loaf of bread, he was overwhelmed with sympathy and glad that he had at least a little food to share with them. He was sure they meant him no harm. When they finished eating, they talked a little as Lazar drove the wagon.

They told him they had escaped from a camp near Bialystok. Hiding days and walking nights, they were trying to make it east to the Front where they hoped to sneak through the German lines and eventually get home. They were all from around Smolensk, about halfway between Minsk and Moscow. They still had a very long way to travel and Lazar didn't have the heart to tell them how many escapees were being recaptured and that every day in Volkovysk he saw them being herded back to camps.

They asked Lazar if there were forests near Volkovysk in which they could hide and Lazar said yes, there was one just on the north edge of town and he would be glad to take them there. He said that they should make it to the woods about daybreak. They wanted to know if he would promise to come back with food later in the morning and he said he would. Once Lazar understood that these were simply tired, hungry and frightened men, he was no longer fearful that they would harm him but he was still afraid they might keep him with them for the horse and wagon and the safety a boy would afford them if German soldiers were around. The promise to get them food would be his chance to get away.

By daybreak, they arrived at the edge of the forest and Lazar stopped the wagon. The men got out, thanked him and told him that they would be waiting for him close to the highway. He watched until they walked into the woods, relieved that he was still in the wagon and they were not. Then he snapped the reins and told the mare: Hurry up, horse, get moving! Let's get home!

... I got home and told my folks what happened and of my promise to the soldiers that I would return with food. Mother said they would not allow me to do it, that it was too risky to take the chance. Later that afternoon, I was walking to the market. I saw the four Russian soldiers. They had been recaptured and were being taken back to prison camp. I didn't let them see me. Perhaps they were better off being recaptured, rather than starving or freezing to death. Or maybe I should have brought them the food. I don't know if they were captured before I would have gotten there with the food or after.

2. ~

Things were not going well for the Germans since the Americans had entered the war and we heard that it wouldn't be long before the war was over. The winter came in strong, with plenty of snow and ice, and I stopped traveling to Bialystok. I did what I could to earn a few Marks here and there. One day a young man hired me to take him by sleigh to a village about thirty-five kilometers from Volkovysk. I didn't question him what for, I was just glad to earn the money.

We arrived there in the afternoon and went to a house where we were welcomed by a man and his wife. They gave us hot tea, bread and butter, and some cheese and milk. Then the two men went out and I was told to wait in the house. The woman started to cook the evening meal. The two men were gone for several hours. For some reason I felt uneasy about the whole thing, even though the house was nice and warm and the woman was friendly.

The two men returned just as it was getting dark. There was a third man with them. When the man I was driving for took off his coat and jacket, I noticed he had a gun in a holster strapped to his waist. As the woman set the table for dinner, the men began to drink vodka. I was scared. But I was also hungry and ate whatever was given to me, hot potato soup with some kind of meat, fresh bread and milk. After dinner my passenger and I started for home . . .

※

Something was very peculiar about all this, but Lazar couldn't put his finger on it. Who was this man and why was he wearing a gun? Guns were nothing new, he saw them all the time, the Germans wore them, and the police, but they were always in uniform and this man was not. And who were the other two men? None of them looked like robbers. And why had they spoken in such low voices to each other that he could barely hear them, let alone make out what they were saying?

They had said practically nothing to Lazar, none of them except the woman during the afternoon but she had become silent once they returned; and ever since this man had noticed Lazar staring at his pistol, he had stopped talking to Lazar altogether, whereas he had been quite friendly on the way out to the village. It was a puzzle, all right. Lazar listened to the sound of the bells jingling from the mare's harness and to the swishing of the runners gliding over the packed snow. It was a sound that usually cheered him, especially on a crisp moonlit night, but not tonight. All he could think about was the identity of his mysterious passenger.

Lazar glanced at him out of the corner of his eye. The young man was staring straight ahead, lost in his own thoughts. It was a handsome face with short dark hair, dark eyes and a thin mustache, but it was a very intense face, high cheekbones, a tight mouth and firmly set jaw. As if in response to Lazar's questions, the young man frowned and, still staring straight ahead, spoke to him in a very serious tone of voice.

"Ty znaesh', kto ia takoi?"

Lazar shook his head. No, he did not know who he was.

"Ia bol'shevik-podpol'shchik, rabotaiu s Trotskim. A ty, koli ne durak, derzhi iazyk za zubami."

The man was telling Lazar that he was an underground agent working for Trotsky, and that if Lazar knew what was good for him, he'd keep quiet about what he had seen. But of course Lazar hadn't really seen anything and had no idea what a Bolshevik might be, nor did he know who Trotsky was, these were names he had never heard before. He knew a threat when he heard one, though, so he promised that he would tell no one and the young man said: Good! and that was the last word spoken between them until they arrived back in Volkovysk.

It was near sunrise when Lazar stopped the sleigh and the young man got out. He stood for a moment, staring intently at Lazar. Then he reached into his coat pocket, handed Lazar some money, rubles not marks, gave a sort of salute and said: To the Revolution! Then he wheeled, walked away quickly and disappeared around the corner. Revolution? Did he say revolution? That was a word Lazar did know and it meant trouble! Whoever this man was and whatever had taken place with the other two men, this was a lot more serious than Lazar had first imagined. But it was late and he wasn't feeling all that well, he'd better just get home and think about it later.

... Let me tell you, I was glad to get rid of him and I thank God we got home without being caught.

The next day I was deathly sick, running a high temperature and vomiting. The doctor came and said I had food poisoning. He gave me some kind of medicine to stop the vomiting, but it didn't help. I finally fell asleep and slept until noon the next day. I stayed in bed the rest of that day, eating very little, and gradually I felt better. The next morning I went out to look for some work.

I was hired by a young lady to drive her to Skidel', which was to the north near Grodna. The lady was in the jewelry business and she had three suitcases. It was about ten hours' ride to Skidel' and I wanted to start out the next morning, but she insisted that we leave right after lunch so she could get there early the next morning. We finally got started about four o'clock. It was very cold and there was a lot of snow on the road. We couldn't travel fast because my horse kept gathering snow on her hooves and I would have to stop periodically and knock it off.

We stopped at an inn on the way and rested for about two hours. It was well after dark when we started out again. Several hours later we were going through a thick forest when suddenly we saw a fire and several men gathered around it. I realized they were Russian soldiers. We both got scared. If we turned around and went back, the inn would be closed. I decided to run for it. I waited until we got close and then whipped my horse and she took off in a full gallop.

My horse was a fast runner and we passed them so fast they couldn't stop us, but my horse kept running and we were approaching a bridge and I would never be able to make the turn at that speed. My horse was running straight for the river! However, God was with us. A German sentry saw that we were out of control and somehow he got in front of us and managed to stop my horse. If not for him, we would have all been in the river.

I told him what had happened to make us run like that and he said that they knew Russian soldiers were in the woods but that they stopped trying to recapture them. He said most of the time they came back to prison camp by themselves because they were hungry and cold. My passenger wanted to give him some money, but he wouldn't take it. I thanked him for saving our lives and I drove on.

We arrived in Skidel' in the morning and I took her to a

small hotel. I got paid for my trip and started back. At the edge of the city I stopped at an inn for some hot breakfast. Then I put my horse in a stall and went to the room reserved for all the balagools, drivers like myself, where I lay down on one of the beds and slept until noon. I had lunch, herring and boiled potatoes with hot tea and black bread. It was a sunny but cold afternoon when I left and headed for home. I was well past the forest before night came and arrived home about two in the morning.

When I got up the next day, I told my parents all about my trip and I also told them that I wasn't going to hire out for any more long-distance trips. I decided to look for work in town for the rest of the winter, but there wasn't much work to be had. The only thing left to do was to go to the woods, steal firewood from the Germans and sell it to the bakeries. It meant going there at night and taking a chance on getting caught, but luck was with me and I didn't get caught. We were thus able to get by and managed to have enough money to buy what we needed. But by now the Revolution was in full force and it was a busy winter.

3. ♭

There had been some political rumors all summer about changes in the government since the Tsar stepped down, but no one bothered very much about politics in Volkovysk. Moscow was a long way off and what people worried about most in Volkovysk was how to make a living. But ever since I had that passenger who said he was an underground Bolshevik agent for Trotsky, I began to hear more and more about the Bolsheviks.

In early November we heard that the Bolsheviks took over Petrograd and the Revolution was in full force. The

Bolsheviks, headed by Lenin and Trotsky, were the Red Army and the old revolutionaries and the tsarists were the White Army. More and more of the Russian Army swung over to the Reds and every day the Bolsheviks were gaining strength. Thousands of the White Russian leaders started to flee from Russia or to turn themselves over to the Germans. When they were caught by the Reds, they were shot on the spot without a trial. Most of the people, especially in the western part of Russia, got behind the Communists and took up arms against the Loyalists. Moscow fell to the Bolsheviks. Lenin took over and declared himself leader of the Revolution. He told the people that his government was now in control of all Russia and he gave an order for the Loyalists to lay down their arms and join the Revolution or be shot. However, in some parts of Russia the Whites continued to fight against the Reds, mostly in the east.

By the middle of November Minsk was taken over by the Reds, and then most of our area and the Ukraine. There was little fighting at the German Front. Now that the Americans were in the war, the Germans were losing and they knew that it was only a matter of time before they would have to get out of Russia. Lenin restored order quickly and the Germans began to fall back with very little fighting. In Volkovysk the Germans tried to grab everything they could lay their hands on to ship to Germany, but when the Bolsheviks drew closer they started to pull out. Everybody hid in their cellars until the fighting stopped. It didn't take long. There was an armistice in December.

The Bolshevik army marched into our city and the soldiers were very friendly, calling everybody *tovarishch*. We had never experienced such friendliness from Russian soldiers. Jews were treated as Russians and we never heard derogatory remarks about Jews from anybody. Once again

144

soldiers were placed in everybody's homes. We had four of them in our house. We got along very well with them.

It was like a new world opened up. Every day someone would get up on a box near the marketplace and talk about the Revolution, and sing the new anthem, and ask the people to fall behind them and help build a new Russia. They asked farmers and peasants to produce bigger crops and raise more livestock. Army personnel started to rebuild the army post and they asked the townspeople to come to work two days a week without pay. My days were Sunday and Thursday. We worked for several months that way and no one minded it.

We were treated very well. They said religion was a thing of the past and so there were no more parades on Sunday to church. But they did not stop those who wanted to go to church or to synagogue. Many people agreed with the Communists and stopped going to church. Business was practically at a standstill. I did very little traveling with my horse and tried to get work in town, whatever I could, but there wasn't much.

In the spring of 1918 a proclamation came out that anyone from the age of sixteen to nineteen who owned a saddle should report to City Hall and be enlisted in the mounted police. Suddenly there was a rush to buy any kind of saddle in the stores. I went looking for one too, but they were all sold out. However, our friend the farmer next door had one lying around, it was an old one and he said I could have it.

I was the last one to get in line. When the captain came to me and asked my age, I told him I was fifteen in January. He told me to step aside with three other boys. Then the four of us were told to report the next morning at the stable behind City Hall. All the rest of the boys were told to leave their saddles and they were marched to the army post. We never saw them again. We found out later that they were taken into the army and sent off to training camp. I was now in the mounted police.

4. ↲

When we reported to the stable the next day, all the saddles from the day before were on the ground and we were each told to pick one. Then we were given horses. Mine was a dapple-gray Siberian about fifteen hands tall. The poor horse was so skinny from lack of food I thought he would die any day. But I got feed for him wherever I could and I took good care of him, so he started to look a lot better. He was a very fast runner and I liked him. He liked me too.

A few days later I was given a rifle and ammunition. Our Captain showed us just once how to use the rifle and that was the extent of our training. We had no uniforms, just a band on our sleeves with *Konnaia Politsiia* printed on it. I felt like a big man when I rode my horse through town with my rifle slung on my back. Frumke kept saying that I should never have joined the mounted police because just as soon as I became sixteen, they would take me into the army. I didn't think so, because I figured they would always need somebody in the mounted police and by that time I would be experienced.

We didn't have much to do in the city, as the local police took care of that. We traveled mostly to the surrounding villages and now and then made arrests. The villagers were required to bring a certain amount of their crops to City Hall, and anyone who didn't we had to arrest. One day an order was issued that anyone who owned a horse must report one day a week for work. I knew that was coming. I quickly dismantled my wagon and hid the wheels. I was about to hide my horse too, but I found out that I was exempt from the work because of my sick father and because I was on duty every day except on Sabbath. I was glad that I didn't have to enforce this law with our neighbors, as that was the job of the local police.

It was the middle of the summer. There was no end to the speeches in the Square, telling the people about the Revolution, about the progress that was being made and what a wonderful life it would be under the Bolshevik Government, and that we must all get solidly behind the Government and do what we were asked. Things were running smoothly in Volkovysk and in the surrounding villages. The big wealthy farms were divided up and the peasants got all the land they could handle. Everybody was required to work the land they were given, keeping a certain amount of their crops and turning over the rest to the Government.

We no longer had soldiers living in our house, they had moved to the army post when the rebuilding was done. Our lives were back to normal again. We wondered how long that would last. In the spring the Bolsheviks had signed a treaty with Germany that recognized the independence of Poland, but in August trouble started to brew in Poland. The Poles wanted the Russians to leave Poland and wanted the Russian border to go back to Minsk. The Bolsheviks were against that.

Suddenly a lot of underground movements started up and the Government began to arrest Poles who spoke out against the Bolsheviks. Now we in the mounted police had a lot of work to do, to travel to the villages and arrest members of the Polish Underground. I was called into my Captain's office one day and told to go home and get to sleep early, because we would be starting out at three in the morning and riding to a village about thirty kilometers from Volkovysk to arrest three men who were Polish organizers . . .

❧

The horses were impatient, stamping about in the dark and chomping nervously on their bits, ignoring the commands of their youthful riders to be quiet and stand still. It was pitch-black and they could hardly see each other. Lazar yawned and tried to rub the sleep from his eyes. He was too tired to be excited. What an ungodly hour to have to get up and go on a mission! Kapitan Zorkov had told them his plan was to get there before sunrise and surprise the three men in their sleep, that way there would be less trouble, but Lazar would sooner have gone in the daytime anyway.

They had been waiting several minutes outside police headquarters for the Captain. Now he was coming out, strapping his holster to his waist as he walked toward them. He was a young man, short but powerfully built, and he had a huge red mustache of which he was inordinately proud, constantly twirling the ends so that they curved upward in a wide sweep that extended out almost even with his ears.

He swung up into his saddle, wheeling his horse around at the same time and shouting over his shoulder for the boys to follow him and stay close together. Then he took off at a fast canter and disappeared into the dark. The boys hurried their horses in an effort to catch up, riding two abreast with Lazar bringing up the rear alone, and for the next hour or so they rode silently and did their best to stay close behind their Captain.

It wasn't easy. It was a very dark night and he was leading them on shortcuts through the fields, the pace too fast for them to see where they were going. The horses were constantly stumbling and it was all they could do to cling to their saddles and keep up with him. This was the Captain's first big mission since taking over the mounted po-

lice and he was obviously determined to show his superiors that he was worthy of their trust and worthy of even more important duties.

All he ever thinks about is his promotion, thought Lazar, this is crazy, somebody's going to get hurt. Just then, the gray stumbled and almost went down. His head dipped and he struggled wildly to regain his balance, planting his hind legs hard and almost stopping dead in his tracks. And Lazar, whose mind had not been where it should have been or his knees would have been pressed a whole lot tighter against his horse's flanks, went flying through the air with a loud Ohhh! and landed a good four meters from his horse. Fortunately, the ground was fairly soft and Lazar landed in a way that his hands and feet helped break the fall.

Nicholas had been closest to Lazar and heard him cry out. He shouted ahead to the Captain that Lazar had been thrown from his horse. Everybody turned and rode back to where Lazar was now brushing himself off, shaken but unhurt, the gray horse calmly standing by, waiting. The Captain was annoyed. He shouted at Lazar to remount and be quick about it, they were losing time! and he took off again at the same mad pace.

It had been getting lighter for some time. The Captain kept glancing nervously toward the eastern sky, obviously upset at running later than his plan. By time they reached the village the sky to the east was streaked with bright hues of red, yellow and orange pushing ahead of the sun. They headed straight for the farmhouse where the three men were reported to be staying.

But the dogs heard them while they were still a long way off and they set up such a racket that it would be a miracle if the people inside still were sleeping. They weren't. As

Lazar and the others approached the farmhouse, the front door opened and several women came out. Standing with their hands on their hips, they watched as two of the boys rode around to cover the rear, the other three spread out in front, their rifles at the ready, and the Captain moved his horse forward until he was almost on top of the women.

He dismounted, shoved his way past the women without a word, and with his pistol drawn entered the house. In a few minutes he came back out with several more women. Eight women now stood in the yard and the young Captain demanded to know where the men were, but it was obvious that they had been warned by the dogs and fled and that none of the women was going to talk. One of the dogs came too close, sniffing at his boot, and he kicked the dog with such force that the dog rolled over twice and ran yowling away toward the barn with his tail between his legs. The Captain was in a foul mood.

He motioned for Lazar and the others to dismount, at the same time shouting instructions to the two in the rear to stand guard outside, one in the back and one in the front with the horses. Then he waved the women back inside with his pistol and said: Come with me! to the boys. Lazar didn't like the sound of his voice, but he hurried after the Captain. He had already received one tongue-lashing when he fell from his horse and didn't particularly relish another. The Captain had a wicked temper and Lazar decided it would be best to humor him, especially since the three men appeared to have escaped and the Captain was going to have to go back empty-handed.

Inside, the women stood together in a tight cluster at the far end of the room in front of the fireplace, their faces clearly showing their fear of this man with the red mustache and drawn pistol. The boys stood just inside the door, rifles cradled in their arms, waiting for instructions. Lazar felt very uncomfortable. He tried to smile and look friendly, thinking the women would be less frightened of him, but they weren't watching him at all, it was the Captain they feared as he stood in front of them, glowering, tapping the barrel of his pistol on the palm of his left hand.

Lazar looked around the room. It was large, but there was very little furniture except for a big table in the middle with ten chairs placed around it. On one side of the room was a high cabinet, a wood stove, and a sink with a water pump next to it. Something was cooking on the stove and it made Lazar's stomach growl. He was getting hungry. On the other side of the room were several mattresses on the floor next to the wall. The doors to two other rooms were ajar and Lazar could see into them from where he stood. They were bedrooms. An old gray cat was sprawled out on the mantel over the fireplace, asleep, oblivious of the tension that now filled the room as the Captain moved slowly from one woman to the next, each time laying the cold barrel of his pistol alongside the woman's cheek and staring fiercely into her frightened eyes.

Lazar glanced at the other boys. They were as nervous as he was, shifting their weight from one leg to the other, not knowing quite what to do except wait to see what the Captain would do next. They're not going to tell him where the men are, Lazar thought, why don't we just leave? What's he up to anyway, why doesn't he say something?

The Captain had returned to the third woman, a young blonde about twenty years old and very pretty. He stood in front of her for several minutes, caressing her with the barrel of his pistol, up and down her cheek and neck, inside the neckline of her dress, fluffing out her long blond hair with it, until at last she was blushing beet-red. He smiled. It was not a friendly smile. I just wish we'd leave, Lazar thought. Then the Captain grabbed the young

151

woman by the hand and strode quickly toward one of the bedrooms, pulling her along behind him. He beckoned toward the women with his head and told the boys: Watch them! Then he slammed the door shut.

The other two boys uncradled their rifles and held them ready, watching the women as they had been commanded. Lazar just stared at the closed door. The women glanced at each other but said nothing and made no move away from the fireplace. Lazar continued to stare at the closed door and wondered why the Captain had chosen to question the young woman separately from the other women. As the answer began to occur to him, he had a sinking feeling in his stomach. Surely he wasn't going to . . . ?

A scream came from the room, and then another. Lazar's comrades took two steps toward the women and pointed their rifles menacingly. Oh no, Lazar said under his breath, oh my god! There were no further sounds from the bedroom. They stood there in silence, the seven women by the fireplace, the three boys with rifles by the door, and everyone knew what was going on in the bedroom, and no one did anything about it. I wish I had never joined the mounted police, Lazar thought, I wish there were no wars, I wish . . . .

Finally the bedroom door opened. The Captain came out first, all serious and official, barking orders to the boys; the young woman followed, her face ashen, her eyes downcast. Slowly, she walked back to the fireplace. Lazar realized that the women no longer appeared frightened. They were seething with anger and loathing and as they stared at the Captain, their eyes were filled with hatred. Still they made no move and they said nothing.

The Captain ordered the two boys outside to stand guard over the house and let no one out. He told Lazar and the other two to come with him. They mounted their horses and rode off in search of the three men. For two hours they searched through the small village and the surrounding fields and woods. It was a fruitless search. Meanwhile, the Captain's temper seemed to have abated and he persisted in recounting his sexual exploit to his "men," how he had raped her three times and how she had resisted him the first time but not the other two.

"Posmotret' na neë, ona byla vpolne dovol'na," he told them with a grin, she looked like she was entirely satisfied. And then he laughed.

Lazar wasn't listening. The whole thing had made him sick to his stomach and he felt like throwing up, but he was afraid to for fear the Captain would be angry or the others would laugh at him. He was also very apprehensive about the men for whom they searched. What if we do find them, will there be a fight? He didn't want to shoot anybody, and he didn't want to be shot either. He wished he had never joined up, that's all. Behind every tree and bush he expected to see a man pop out with a rifle pointing straight at him. He held his rifle tightly across his lap, unconsciously moving his finger on and off the trigger.

Shots! Rifle shots! Lazar flinched, but realized that it wasn't coming from the woods. It's coming from the farmhouse, yelled the Captain, come on! They turned and raced in the direction of the farmhouse. Suddenly Lazar's horse stumbled and nearly lost his footing. Lazar's hand instinctively tightened on the rifle, his finger on the trigger, and the gun went off with a loud Bang! The bullet whizzed right by the Captain, barely missing him as it tore through his coat leaving two small holes.

The Captain was furious. He began to scream at Lazar, who felt faint and started to cry. Sobbing, he tried to explain what happened, how his horse had stumbled and the gun had gone off accidentally, at the same time trying desperately to stop crying and to keep from falling off the horse because of the dizziness. The Captain continued to rave. Put it on your shoulder, you idiot! Never ride with a gun on your lap! You could have killed me! Son of a whore! He was beside himself, yelling a string of oaths only half of which Lazar had even heard before, much less understood.

Then the Captain, remembering at last the shots they had heard coming from the farmhouse, threw one hand up in the air dismissing the matter, turned and galloped off toward the farmhouse with the other two boys closely behind him and Lazar trailing far in the rear. It was all too much for him to deal with. It's your fault, he muttered to the gray horse, but he knew that it wasn't, not really, he simply didn't belong here. Mother and Father would be very upset if they knew what was going on. It made Lazar feel very guilty.

When he reached the others at the farmhouse, the two boys were explaining that the women had made an attempt to leave the house and they had fired in the air to let the women know they would carry out their orders if they had to. The Captain was pleased. He seemed in a good mood again and appeared to have forgotten all about the accidental shooting. It was past noon and the Captain was hungry. He ordered the women to prepare lunch for them.

After a lunch of kalbasse, eggs, cheese, goat's milk and fresh black bread, the boys taking turns eating and standing guard, the Captain said he was going to take a nap, that they should be alert on guard and in case the men returned or the women tried to escape, they should wake him immediately. Then he stretched out on one of the mattresses on the floor, his pistol in his hand and resting on his chest, and soon he was snoring through his big red mustache.

About four o'clock the Captain woke up and announced to the women that since they had refused to give him information as to the whereabouts of their men, they were all under arrest and he was taking them to police head-

*quarters in Volkovysk. He went off with Nicholas to get
two wagons in the village, leaving Lazar with the women
and the other two standing guard outside. Lazar pleaded
with the women to tell the Captain something, anything,
just so they wouldn't have to go to jail. He also apologized
for what had happened in the morning, but explained that
he and the others were under the Captain's orders and
didn't dare disobey him. They said they understood, that it
was the Captain they hated, not the boys, but there was
nothing they could do, they too were under orders.*

*The women prepared clothes and food for the journey.
Lazar watched them and thought of Mother and Frumke.
Suppose the situation had been reversed? Suppose it had
been Frumke who had been raped and Mother who had
had to stand by and do nothing about it? And suppose it
had been he and Father who were hiding out in the woods
while that was going on? German soldiers had lived in his
house, and Russian soldiers too, and they had always
treated his mother and sister with respect; and yet, here he
was, involved in something like this and doing nothing to
stop the Captain.*

*Lazar was very tired. This job was not at all the way he
had imagined it would be when he first rode down the
street, so proud on his gray horse with a rifle on his back,
and he was ashamed that he had volunteered. He wondered if they would let him quit when he got back, or
would they just throw him into the army?*

*"I'm sorry," he said out loud again, "I'm very sorry."
None of the women paid any attention to him. He was just
a boy trying to be a man, and they had work to do.*

. . . It was dark out when we started to travel. After we
left the village, someone must have gotten the information
to the men in their hideout. We heard rifle shots and we
could tell the men were following us. The night was very

dark. We couldn't see anyone, but they kept shooting at us and we returned shots in the air. We stopped several times so the Captain could put his ear to the ground to hear if they were on horses or following us on foot. He yelled out several times: If you want your women, give yourselves up and we will let them go home! but there was no response.

We were getting close to our city and there were no more shots. I was glad the nightmare was over. We got to the police station about two in the morning. The women were put into jail. The Captain somehow managed to take the girl with him to his room. The next day we did not question him about the girl and he didn't mention anything about her. After two days of questioning, they let the women go home, all but one. I don't know what became of her.

The Captain had to make out his report about his failure to capture the three men. He was not very happy about that. From that time on we were not sent out on that kind of mission again. All I had to do was ride from village to village to check with the farmers and see that they delivered the Government's share of their crops. That was fine with me, I had enough of shooting and being shot at.

Chapter Eight

1. ꜰ

There was a lot of fighting going on in Russia. The Red Army was still fighting the White Army, especially in the east, and now fighting was breaking out with the Poles in the west. The Bolsheviks had agreed to recognize Poland in a treaty Trotsky signed with Germany in the spring, but Poland wanted the Russians out of their country and the borders moved back to Minsk.

The Bolsheviks were weak and weary from four years of war, and now the Revolution. They fell back before the Polish advance and once again we were faced with the possibility of fighting in Volkovysk. I was worried that the Bolsheviks would make me come with them and that they wouldn't let me stay home with my family.

Our Polish neighbor's son, Nikol, who had been a prisoner of war in a German camp, was released and allowed to come home to work the fields with his father who was over seventy. Nikol was about forty, a very strong man about six feet tall with blond hair and a small reddish beard. Nikol had been in the Russian Army since the war began; now he said he would be willing to serve in the Polish Army because this time he would be fighting for his

Fatherland. He had a wife and two children and he felt very strongly about being Polish. I liked Nikol. I had known him ever since I was old enough to walk and talk.

In the early part of the spring Nikol's father had given us two acres of his field in which to plant our potatoes. It was about the third week in September and getting time to dig them out before the freeze, but fighting had begun around our city and we decided to wait. On the second day of the fighting I was in the stable and my Captain said to get ready, we were going to pull out. Suddenly there was a burst of firing and people started to run out of City Hall. I decided it was a good chance to run home.

I ran between the houses until I got home, but I was afraid the Captain would come looking for me. I told my family to hide my horse in the kitchen of our empty apartment and to say they didn't know where I was. Then I hid out in Nikol's barn. The fighting lasted all day and night. I stayed in the loft on top of the straw. Sometimes I could hear bullets whizzing by where I was hiding. The next morning, Polish soldiers marched in and took over the city. Nikol called out to tell me it was safe for me to go home.

We were under still another new regime. People went out in the streets to welcome the soldiers, but this time we found them very unfriendly and they would shove and push anyone in their way. We had heard that the Poles from around Warsaw and north of Warsaw were the worst anti-Semites and they showed it. One morning I walked to the market and was on the sidewalk when three soldiers walked toward me. As they passed, one soldier slapped my face so hard that it spun me around. He told me to get off the sidewalk, that Jews had no right to walk on the sidewalk.

It was very difficult for a while, especially for Jews, but soon the soldiers moved on and things started to get normal. City Hall was now run by the Poles and they attempted to establish law and order. Occasionally Polish soldiers would pass through town and then it was dangerous for anybody to be caught in the streets with a horse and wagon. The soldiers would grab the horse and wagon so they could ride to the front lines instead of walk, since they had no transportation of their own. The trains weren't running because the Russians had blown up the bridges.

In the first week of October, Mother, Frumke and I started to dig up the potatoes. Nikol was near us plowing up his own potatoes and when he finished, he came over to help us. As he was plowing our potatoes up, two Polish soldiers came and they demanded that he give them his horse. He took his horse and started to run away. They yelled for him to stop and he didn't. They shot at him and I saw him fall to the ground. I ran to help him. He was shot through the right thigh and bleeding badly.

I told the soldiers that Nikol was Polish and that they couldn't have his horse because I had to use it to take him to the hospital. They took off. I harnessed his horse to my wagon and rushed to the hospital, but he died on the way. His wife had been with us when this happened. She cried and screamed that he had come home from the war without a scratch and now their own people had killed him. It was a terrible experience.

Nikol's funeral was two days later. The whole Polish community turned out. His family searched for the two soldiers, but there was no trace of them. Several days went by and I had all our potatoes in the cellar. Winter set in and there was nothing to do. There was no work. I decided to sell my horse but could find no one to give me my price. People were afraid to buy horses because the soldiers would take them if you showed up on the street with a horse. I continued to keep my horse in the kitchen of our empty apartment.

Christmas holidays arrived and we could hear church

bells again. It was the first time in a long while that they had been rung. The spirit of Christmas was in the streets and houses. We didn't see many soldiers passing through anymore and the Polish Government seemed to have better control now. Everybody thought that we would have some peace for a while.

We had a letter from America pleading with us to come, but my father wouldn't hear of it. He refused even to discuss it. Things were hard, but my parents were too proud to ask their children in America for help. I was getting fed up with all the war and with all the responsibility on my shoulders for making a living and trying to support my family. I wished my father would change his mind about going to America, but it seemed he never would.

2. ♭

In the spring of 1919 my old Polish friend and protector from school, Gregori, turned eighteen and to avoid being drafted into the army, he joined the local police force. I saw him sometimes in his uniform, and he was very proud and acted as if he were the most important official in town.

By that time the soldiers were no longer passing through Volkovysk and grabbing horses off the street, so I was able to take my horse out of the apartment and put her back in her stall. I started to look for work again. Meanwhile, the local police were going from house to house and telling those who owned horses that they must work for the city one day a week for no pay. One morning, just as I was getting ready to leave with my horse and wagon because I had a job that day, Gregori showed up to tell me I had to work for the city.

I told him that I had earned no money all winter and

that I finally got a job for the day that would pay good money, and that I would work for the city the next day instead. But Gregori had to show me what a big man he was, that he was important and I was not, and he insisted I would have to report for work that day or he would arrest me. I couldn't believe it was the same Gregori who used to be my friend.

As we were arguing in front of the house, my father came out and stood in front of the horse and wagon, holding my horse's harness, and he told Gregori that I was not going to work for the city that day because I had already promised the baker I would work for him. Then Gregori got mad and he hit my father very hard across the chest with the butt of his rifle. My father fell down and Gregori must have been scared because he took off.

I went to City Hall to complain to the Polish officials about Gregori hitting my father, but it didn't do any good. I was told that I must join the other wagons and go to work. I saw Gregori at the police station and I told him don't you ever come to my house again. Father was ill for several days after that, complaining of chest pains. I was never so angry at anyone in my life. I think if I had had a gun that day Gregori hit my father, I would have shot him.

I saw his father in the street several days later and I told him what Gregori did to my father. He was shocked that his son would do something like that and promised that he would have Gregori ask my father for forgiveness. I told him that I had told his son never to come to my house again and I meant it. He apologized and said he would see to it that Gregori bothered us no more. I never saw Gregori again.

There was now a big shortage of horses in Volkovysk. Dealers were buying all the horses they could get and paying good prices for them. I could have gotten a good price for my mare, but I didn't want to sell her unless I could get another. I bumped into Moishe and Boris at the market one day and Moishe told us that his father had overheard a customer in their tearoom saying there were plenty of horses available in Slonim, that dealers were bringing them across the Russian border and selling them in Slonim for very reasonable prices.

The three of us decided we should go to Slonim to buy three horses and bring them back to Volkovysk where we could sell them for a good profit. We talked it over with our parents and they all approved, so the next day we set out for Slonim with over six hundred rubles between us . . .

Lazar was excited about going to Slonim with Boris and Moishe.ᵉ It was like the old days on the farm when they worked together. The last few months had been boring. No more traveling, no more adventures. Sure, he had been frightened sometimes on the road, but he had been excited too and he missed that excitement. Hanging around town all winter looking unsuccessfully for work had been pretty dull. And there hadn't been anything else to do.

He was itchy to make some money, too. Making money made Lazar feel important. If he didn't make money, he felt useless. Besides, one apartment was empty again, which made whatever Lazar brought in that much more important. Lazar reached into his pocket and felt the tight roll of old bills held together with a wide rubber band, all one hundred and eighty-five rubles his mother had been saving for months in her "pushka," and he smiled. If things went well, he might just double that for her in the next few days, wouldn't she and Father be pleased if he managed that!

The three boys were stretched out on a mound of fresh-

*cut hay, their legs dangling over the back edge of a farm-
er's wagon headed for Zel'na, about two-thirds of the way
to Slonim, Boris puffing on a new pipe, Moishe smoking a
cigarette, and Lazar holding a thick piece of straw in his
mouth as if it were a cigarette because he really couldn't
stand to smoke. Rides had not been plentiful today and
they had had to settle for a number of short ones. This was
the fifth ride of the day and it was almost sundown already. Slow going. Oh well, they were in no hurry. The
trains would be running from Zel'na and they could catch
a train there for Slonim. Then tomorrow they could shop
for the horses.*

*When the farmer reached his turnoff they got out,
thanked him for the ride, and walked the rest of the way to
Zel'na. The train station was easy enough to find, it was
just near the highway on the north end of town, and their
timing was almost perfect. They caught the last train to
Slonim with half an hour to spare.*

*The trains were still crowded with military personnel,
but civilians were allowed to ride whenever there was
space. No one else seemed to be going from Zel'na and the
boys were able to find themselves some room to sit in the
corner of one of the cars. A few soldiers looked them over
and asked where they were going, Slonim, they answered,
but nothing else was said and they were left alone.*

*About ten P.M. the train stopped at a station and the boys
got off, thinking they had arrived in Slonim. As they
walked away from the train, Lazar said, "This isn't
Slonim. I think we got off at the wrong station!"*

*They raced back, but the train had already started
again, the doors were closed and there was no way to get
back on. It was no real problem, they were so close to
Slonim they could walk the rest of the way. The whole
thing struck them as very funny and they laughed uproar-
iously at their own stupidity. As they left the platform,*

still laughing, two Polish military policemen stopped them and demanded to see their papers. Something about the way the soldiers now barred their passage made them nervous and they stopped laughing immediately.

None of the boys had identification. What were you doing on that train? they were asked, and they answered that they were on their way to Slonim from Volkovysk to buy horses. One of the soldiers stared intently at Boris. You are all under arrest, he said, and he ordered them to come with him.

The boys were thoroughly confused. Under arrest? What for? They hadn't done anything! They had got off the train by mistake, were now walking to Slonim where they were going to buy some horses in the morning, there was no law against that! This didn't make sense. One soldier led the way, the other followed behind, pushing Boris with his rifle whenever he fell behind the others. Shut up! No talking! Move along!

They were taken to a large gray frame house two squares from the railroad station. Several more military policemen stood around in front of the house and on the porch. It appeared to Lazar that this must be a headquarters of some kind. Inside the house, they were told to wait. One soldier guarded them while the other knocked twice on a door and then entered, closing the door behind him. He came out in a few minutes and motioned the boys inside.

Two men were in the room, standing behind a desk at the far end. The room was dark except for a floor lamp next to the desk, twisted so that it pointed away from the desk and toward the door. Lazar blinked at the brightness of the light. He couldn't see the two men clearly, only the dark outline of their bodies, but he could tell they were in uniforms. There was one wooden chair in front of the desk and what looked like two or three more behind the desk. There appeared to be no other furniture in the room. Lazar

*had the feeling that there was a third man in the far
corner of the room, but it was too dark to be certain. It was
a very large room.*

*One of the men spoke in Polish, telling the boys to come
forward and empty their pockets onto the desk. As they
were doing that, he asked Boris where he had gotten the
coat he was wearing. It was an old army coat that Boris
had bought a few weeks before in the market. Boris was
frightened by the tone of the man's voice and he answered
haltingly that he had bought it in the market in Volkovysk
for two rubles and that he thought it must have been left
behind by a Bolshevik soldier along with a great many
other supplies discarded by the Bolsheviks when they
pulled out of Volkovysk just before the Polish soldiers arrived.*

*Where is the bill of sale, the man demanded. Boris of
course had no bill of sale. Even if there had been one, he
would hardly be carrying it around with him, not for an
old army coat for two rubles, for god's sake! But he didn't
say that, he was by now too frightened even to talk, he just
shrugged and shook his head.*

*The man pounded his fist on the desk, yelled for the sol-
dier outside the door who came in immediately, and told
him to take Lazar and Moishe to another room while he
questioned Boris. The two boys were taken to an empty
room adjacent to the one in which they had just been, and
they stayed there for perhaps an hour. They could hear Boris
screaming out in pain and crying.*

"My god, they're beating him!" whispered Moishe.

*"It must be the coat," answered Lazar, "they kept look-
ing at his coat. Why did he have to wear that coat anyway?
What are they doing to him?"*

*Lazar and Moishe were terrified. Boris's screaming next
door was almost continuous now. This whole thing was
like a bad dream! One minute they were all laughing be-*

cause they got off the train at the wrong station and the next minute they were under arrest and being beaten up by Polish military police! For what?

The screaming stopped. They could hear Boris whimpering like a small child. They heard the door of the office open, footsteps coming down the hall, Boris's whimpering growing closer. The door to the room opened and Boris was shoved into the dark room with such force that he staggered, tripped, and finally fell in a sobbing heap at Lazar's feet. Blood trickled from the corner of his mouth, two front teeth were missing and his right eye was badly bruised. In the light coming from the hall, Lazar could see a huge red welt that ran straight across Boris's face, starting at the right ear, extending across the bridge of his nose and his left cheek to the other ear. Boris looked awful.

The soldier stood in the doorway grinning and motioned for Lazar. It was his turn. For a moment Lazar felt dizzy. His legs were quivering and he couldn't seem to feel his feet. He took a deep breath, tried to smile at Moishe and walked around Boris toward the door. The sound of his own footsteps were deafening and he could hear himself breathing very heavily. There was a ringing in his ears and he fought to keep from fainting. Maybe they will only ask me questions, he thought, after all, I'm not the one wearing a Russian Army coat.

The soldier grabbed him roughly by the back of his neck, shoved him into the room with the two men and slammed the door shut. The two men were sitting behind the desk. The chair in front of the desk had been placed directly under the lamp. One of the men was pouring himself some vodka. The other, the man who had asked Boris about the coat, smiled at Lazar and motioned for him to sit in the chair.

Lazar sat down. The man was still smiling. He took a long puff on his cigarette, inhaled deeply and blew it out.

He got up from his chair, came around to the front of the desk and leaned against it, his left hand hooked in his belt. He looked at Lazar and smiled again. Lazar smiled back. Maybe this wasn't going to be so bad after all. The man seemed friendly enough. Maybe he would just ask some questions and Lazar could explain who he was and about the horses in Slonim.

The man took another long puff on his cigarette, inhaled and blew the smoke slowly into Lazar's face. Lazar coughed. Still looking straight at Lazar and smiling, the man reached to his right and stubbed his cigarette out in the ashtray. Lazar smiled again, awkwardly, not knowing quite what to say or do. The man nodded, still smiling, and swung his fist in a wide arc from the ashtray, catching Lazar square on the chin and sending him flying out of his chair to the floor.

Blood spurted from a cut on Lazar's mouth, his ears rang with the noise of the man's fist colliding with his jaw, his vision was momentarily blurred and he had trouble focusing. He wasn't even aware of what had just happened, only of a loud crunching noise and the terrible jarring impact of something banging into his face, and now the slowly spreading pain in his jaw and neck. It all happened so fast! The man had been smiling, and Lazar had been completely disarmed by the warmth of the man's smile and smiled back. He had no idea what hit him!

Before he fully understood what had just happened, Lazar felt the man grab his shirt and sweater at the chest with one hand, lift him off the floor and slam him back into the chair.

"Przyznaj się!" he snarled, no longer smiling. "My wiemy, ty jestes szpiegiem! Kto cie przystat?" (Confess! We know you are a spy. Who sent you?)

Lazar answered in Polish, doing his best not to cry, his jaw hurting and his lip slightly numb which interfered

*with his speech. "Proszę, Pana, ja nie jestem szpiegiem."
(Please, Sir, I am not a spy.)*

*The man behind the desk continued to sip his vodka,
lighting a cigarette, while the first man slapped Lazar's
face, hard, first with his palm, then with the back of his
hand, again and again, shouting, "Przyznaj się, szpiegiem!
Kto cię przytat?"*

*Lazar was crying now. Over and over he sobbed that he
was not a spy, that he was on his way to Slonim to buy a
horse. Dimly, he became aware that there was indeed another man sitting in the corner, he could see the red glow
of a cigarette, but there was no time to speculate as to who
it might be, the man in front of him was occupying all his
attention. Once again he pleaded for the man to stop, in-
sisting that he was not a spy.*

*The man reached over and grabbed Lazar's shirt and
sweater again, pulling him half out of his chair until their
faces almost touched and Lazar could smell the mixture of
vodka and tobacco on his breath. Still holding Lazar's
clothes, he dragged Lazar to the door, opened the door
halfway, shoved Lazar's fingers into the crack at the back
edge of the door near the hinges and pushed the door
closed slowly with his foot.*

*The crack narrowed and Lazar's fingers were pinched
between the door and the frame. As the man pushed his
foot harder against the door, Lazar screamed out in agony
and fell to his knees. The man pulled him to his feet again,
pushing even harder on the door. The pain was unbearable.*

"Talk, you Bolshevik Jew son of a bitch!"

*But all Lazar could answer was: "My name is Lazar Un-
ovitch. I am from Volkovysk. I am not a spy!"*

*Lazar was only vaguely aware of the pain in his hand.
His thinking had slowed down considerably. It was only
as he was being dragged back to the chair that he even
realized his hand was no longer being squeezed by the*

door and only then that he heard the door being kicked shut moments before. Had he passed out? He wasn't sure.

The second man came around from behind the desk. He reached over and gently took Lazar's hand in his own, as though he intended to examine it under the light. Lazar watched as the man took the cigarette from his mouth with his other hand and deliberately stubbed it out on the back of his injured hand. He saw the black spot form on his hand, an angry red spreading around it, and he heard the sizzling of his own burning hair and flesh, but it was a long time before he felt the pain. Then a brand-new pain burst through the dull throbbing of his fingers and exploded in his brain and Lazar screamed! The man chuckled.

The man behind the desk poured himself a glass of vodka. For the next half hour the two men took turns smacking Lazar and yelling at him. They continued to drink. One bottle was emptied. Another opened. Lazar's jaw and hand throbbed with pain. He screamed out the names of every Polish family he could remember who might know him in Volkovysk. He wasn't a spy! People knew him in Volkovysk! His name was Lazar Unovitch!

Suddenly, something hard hit Lazar on the back of the head and he blacked out. When he came to, he was lying on the floor. Water was being poured on his head. Hands reached under his armpits and lifted him back to the chair. He was still dizzy. He had a terrible headache. He felt his boots and socks being taken off. The first man straddled his legs and grabbed them under the calves. His feet were now off the floor and bare. The second man removed his belt and held it in his right hand, doubled in half with the two ends loosely together and the belt buckle dangling. Slowly, he tapped the ends against his open palm.

"What are their names?" asked the man with the belt. "Give us the names and we will let you go."

Lazar couldn't focus on what was being asked of him. He barely heard the words; he couldn't put them together. He gazed dully at the man.

Whack! The belt struck the bottoms of his feet, the buckle stabbing through the skin on his right foot. Lazar was plunged into a new and horrible pain. Whack! Whack! Whack! Again and again. The soles of his feet were bleeding and on fire.

Lazar screamed and screamed, choking on his saliva, his face contorted by pain. "Please don't hit me anymore! Please don't hit me anymore!"

At last the beating stopped. Lazar was ordered to stand up, pick up his boots and socks and go back to the other room. He tried to comply, but it was impossible for him to stand. He crawled on his hands and knees toward the door, his boots in one hand, his socks in the other. Twice he was kicked from behind by a heavy boot and sent sprawling, and the soldiers laughed, but it made no difference to Lazar. He felt nothing from the kick, no pain at all, and he couldn't have cared less what they did to him anymore. He had passed over the edge of his endurance. His whole body was one elaborate pain. The soldiers must have sensed it and they let Lazar go. For some reason, Lazar found himself wondering who the man was who was sitting in the dark corner.

Lazar sat on the floor, moaning. Boris was next to him, curled on his side and crying. He had had an infection in his bladder the week before and it was bothering him again. He had to go to the bathroom. He didn't know what to do. Lazar was in so much pain that he couldn't talk, but through his pain he worried about Moishe who was in the next room. He prayed that Moishe would be all right.

Occasionally, he could hear Moishe cry out, but it seemed to Lazar that Moishe was not having too hard a

170

time of it. Maybe the soldiers were getting tired. It was late. They had drunk a lot of vodka. And the boys all had the same answers. Maybe they would just realize that he and Boris and Moishe were who they said they were and not spies at all.

They didn't keep Moishe long. When he was brought back, he wasn't hurt badly, just bleeding slightly from a cut on his lip. Lazar had gotten the worst of it with his feet. At least the others could walk. The guard ordered them to come with him and they were taken next door to an empty house and locked in a small basement room. Boris and Moishe helped Lazar, who could barely walk even with most of his weight on their shoulders.

The room was pitch-dark. They heard the key turn in the lock and then the footsteps of the soldier receding, up the basement stairs, across the floor above them, and out the front door. Silence. Boris started to cry. His bladder hurt. Lazar asked Moishe what had happened with him in the other room. He said only one of the men even bothered with him, the other was too drunk and too tired. After hitting him eight or ten times, the man gave up and decided to call it a night.

"You were lucky to be last," said Lazar.

"I know," Boris agreed, "they half-killed you."

Neither Boris nor Moishe was aware of a third man in the room. They were surprised that Lazar had seen someone. Well, not exactly seen him, felt him would be more like it. The only sign he had that someone was there was the glowing cigarette in the corner and he was no longer sure he had even seen that, but there was no doubt in Lazar's mind that there was a third man and that he had been watching everything that took place.

The boys had been whispering, but realized finally that there was no one to hear them, the house was deserted. They began to speak in normal tones. Gradually, their eyes were becoming adjusted to the dark. A thin slit of a win-

dow high up on the outside wall permitted a small amount of light into the room, probably from the headquarters next door, and it was enough to see each other and make out the room they were in.

It was a tiny storage room, about two meters by three, with a wood floor and shelves along one wall. The ceiling was high and consisted of the joists and floor above. There was no glass in the window and the night air blowing in was cold and drafty. The boys talked briefly about escape, but quickly dismissed the idea. The window was too small, the door too thick, and Lazar too crippled to run.

They must know we're not spies by now, they agreed, and they'll no doubt let us go in the morning. Boris took off the old army coat and covered Lazar's feet with it. At least the damn coat could serve some useful purpose, he said, after causing so much trouble. Lazar and Moishe sat on the floor in the corner under the shelves, staying close together to keep warm. Boris was pacing the floor in the dark. Finally he could hold it in no longer. He went to the corner furthest from his friends and urinated. A large puddle of urine spread out over half the floor of the tiny room. Boris came back to the corner under the shelves and sat down with Lazar and Moishe.

"I'm awfully sorry, friends, I just had to piss, I couldn't hold it in any longer. It's this damn infection, it burns and hurts like hell. I should be all right until morning, I'll try anyway."

Lazar and Moishe were too worn out to care one way or the other. It had been a long hard day and they hurt all over. There was no room now for any of them to lie down, the room having been made considerably smaller by Boris's puddle, so the three sat huddled together in the corner to keep warm, heads on each other's shoulders, and at last they all fell asleep.

It seemed only minutes later when they were awakened by the sound of the key turning in the lock and the door banging open. Lazar opened his eyes. Sunlight was streaming in through the tiny windows and a Polish military policeman was standing in the doorway, glaring at the puddle of urine that covered most of the floor. Who did that? he demanded to know, and Boris answered that he did because he was sick and couldn't help it. The soldier ordered him to take off his shirt and wipe it up and be quick about it!

Moishe asked if they could please go to the outhouse when Boris finished cleaning the floor. The soldier grunted affirmatively. Lazar ached all over. His feet were covered with dried blood and cracked from where the soldier's belt buckle had broken the skin the night before. He took off his undershirt and tore it into wide strips which he used to bandage his feet. Then he managed to get his boots back on. Boris finished cleaning the floor as best he could and, gingerly holding the urine-soaked shirt out in front of him with two fingers, he looked at his friends with a sheepish grin made almost ludicrous by his badly swollen face. The three of them made it to the outhouse in the rear of the house, Lazar limping badly and leaning heavily on Moishe for support.

The soldier leaned against the back of the house, smoking and watching. It wasn't likely they were in any shape to run away, especially the young one with the sore feet, but it wouldn't do any harm to keep an eye on them just in case. If they got away the commander would have his hide.

Back in their cell, the boys were given black bread and water for breakfast. Boris asked the soldier why they weren't being released and allowed to go home. Go home? The soldier laughed. He told them they were to be taken to jail in Slonim and tried as Russian spies. He slammed the door shut, locked it, and went back up the stairs still laughing to himself at the joke of spies who said they were boys and wanted to go home to their mamas.

They couldn't help crying. They were still boys, after all,

*not men as they liked to pretend with pipes and cigarettes
and the beginnings of beards, and their situation seemed
so hopeless! To be arrested, beaten, thrown into this basement cell like thieves, fed only stale bread and water, and
now to be told they were going to be tried as spies? Spies
get shot!*

*They sat in their corner and shook their heads in dis-
belief. What could they do? How could they get word to
their parents? This couldn't be true, it couldn't be happening! No one knew where they were. Would their parents be
worried? Would they come looking for them? Would they
find them in time or would they be too late?*

*"God help us," Lazar said, "we've given them the names
of our Polish officials in Volkovysk, won't they check with
them? Would they just put us in jail in Slonim without
even checking with somebody in Volkovysk? Do we really
look like spies or is it just because we're Jews? God help
us!"*

*No one knew the answer to Lazar's questions. They sat
and talked and cried and talked some more, but there
didn't seem any way out of this. They were trapped and
there was absolutely no one who could help them. Over-
come with fatigue and lack of sleep, aching from their
beatings and drained by their fears, the three dozed off
again. Occasionally, one would moan in his sleep or wake
with a start, see the other two sleeping, go back to sleep
again.*

*Lazar woke up. Boris and Moishe were still sleeping. It
must be almost noon, he thought. Mother would be ready-
ing the noon meal. Soup probably, some vegetables and
sour cream, maybe a little herring, fresh bread and butter.
He tried to picture what they looked like, see them moving
about the house, but he couldn't. His feet hurt and his jaw
was sore and all he could picture was the soldier last night,
holding the belt in one hand and tapping it in the palm of*

the other. His eyes filled with tears again. What good is crying, he thought. What good is telling the truth, they don't believe us anyway. What good is anything?

The key turned in the lock and the door opened. Lazar nudged his sleeping friends awake. They watched as a man in a dark suit and hat entered the room and quietly closed the door behind him. He held the key in his hand. He was an older man with a trim gray beard and round glasses. His white shirt was buttoned at the neck, he wore no tie. He looks Jewish, Lazar thought, and there is something about him that seems familiar. But Lazar couldn't place it.

The man stood inside the door looking at the boys, shaking his head and making little tching noises with his tongue on the roof of his mouth. He dropped the key into his pocket and began to speak to the boys in Russian but with a strange accent they had never heard before.

"My name is Mr. Abraham. I have read the report of the military police in which you are accused of being spies. It is their intention to take you to Slonim where you will be put in jail until your trial. However, I do not believe you are Russian spies. I have had tea in your father's tearoom."

He was looking at Moishe. How does he know which of us has a father with a tearoom? wondered Lazar. The man continued in a soft voice.

"I have succeeded in convincing them that you are not spies, that you are instead three Jewish boys from Volkovysk on your way to Slonim to buy horses . . ."

"That's what we told them!" Moishe interrupted excitedly. "But they wouldn't believe us!"

"And they beat us up!" Boris joined in. "They hit me all over and they used a strap on Lazar's feet and . . ."

Mr. Abraham held his hand up for them to be quiet and Boris trailed off in the middle of his sentence, embarrassed.

175

"What can we do now?" Lazar asked.

"Good question," said Mr. Abraham. He seemed to think for a moment. "Are you willing to lose your money and be sent home by train?"

The boys looked at each other. It was money their parents had saved for a long time. But what choice did they have? It was lose the money or chance losing their lives. They all nodded to Mr. Abraham. Anything to get out of this place.

"Very well, I'll see what I can do." Without another word, Mr. Abraham turned and left the room, locking the door behind him.

For almost two hours the boys waited impatiently for Mr. Abraham to return. They were so excited about the prospect of going home that they forgot all about their aches and pains, Boris with his eye swollen shut and two front teeth missing, Moishe with his lower lip twice its normal size, and Lazar who could hardly walk and had a lump on the back of his head the size of a large walnut, not to mention his swollen hand, and they sat in the corner whispering excitedly about their defender, Mr. Abraham.

Who was this strange man with the unusual name and accent? Where had he come from? Why was he helping them? How did he come to have the key to their cell, that he could let himself in and out without a guard accompanying him? But they had no answers, only questions. No matter. Whoever Mr. Abraham was, if he could get them out of here, he was an angel of God!

Someone was at the door again. It was the guard. He told them they were to come with him. There was no sign of Mr. Abraham. Now what? The guard led them back to headquarters. He stopped at the door to the room in which they had been beaten the night before, knocked twice, then opened the door and stood aside. The boys went in and the guard shut the door.

176

Except for the sunlight coming through the windows be-hind the desk, the room was exactly the same. The man who had beat on Lazar's feet with his belt was sitting at the desk. He had on a fresh uniform with the tunic but-toned and he looked very official. He must be the head man, Lazar thought, but if he's the head man, who's Mr. Abraham? It was a puzzle.

Mr. Abraham was in the room. He was sitting in the corner where Lazar had seen the glow of a cigarette the night before. His legs were stretched out and casually crossed at the ankles, his hands were in the pockets of his jacket. A cigarette dangled from his lips and his eyes were half-closed against the smoke curling up from the ciga-rette. He was staring out the window. Not once did he change that position the whole time the boys were in the room.

Without looking up, the officer began to read from the paper in his hand. It was the report on their arrest and "in-terrogation." The report ended with the conclusion that in the opinion of the interrogating officer, the prisoners were Bolshevik spies and the recommendation was that they be tried as enemies of the State. When he finished reading the report he looked up.

He looked at each boy in turn, but without expression. Then he lit a cigarette, picked up another piece of paper and continued. This time he was not reading from the pa-per but was instead talking about it. Mr. Abraham had vouched for them and had given his personal assurance that they were not spies. They would sign a release, he said, and he would guarantee them safe passage back to Volko-vysk plus fifty rubles each for the train.

"We will keep the rest of your money to cover damages," he concluded with a smile.

Then he turned the paper around, placed it on the desk facing the boys and held out a pen. Each of the boys signed their name at the bottom of the paper without read-

ing it. Lazar was the last to sign. He handed back the pen. The officer then tore up the report from which he had read, throwing the pieces into a metal basket on the floor. He placed the paper they had signed into a folder and put the folder in a drawer. From the same drawer he drew out three piles of fifty rubles each and placed them on the desk in front of the boys. Next, he scrawled his signature on a safe conduct pass and put that on top of one of the piles of bills. That done, he turned back to his work.

The boys stood there waiting, wondering what to do. Without looking up from his work, the officer waved his hand and dismissed them with: "You may go. You are free."

Hurriedly, the boys picked up the bills and the safe conduct pass and headed for the door. Lazar glanced back at Mr. Abraham. A long gray ash hung from the end of his cigarette. He was still staring out the window.

As the boys reached the door and opened it, Mr. Abraham spoke at last. "Nie wracaj " he said in a strangely accented Polish. Don't come back.

. . . We were put on the next train for home. We did not see Mr. Abraham again. My feet were still very sore and I could not walk very well. It was just my luck that I was the only one who got that punishment.

We arrived home early the next morning, our faces black and blue, and we had to explain to our parents what had happened to us and to the money. I didn't tell my father the story. When he saw my face and asked what happened, I told him that we had to jump off the train and that I fell hitting my face against some rocks. I don't think he believed me, but he didn't question me further. I didn't tell my mother all the details either. The only one I told the whole story to was Frumke. My mother said that losing the money at a time when it was needed so badly was hard, but that we would manage and that she would thank God for my safe return.

3. ל

Summer came. My feet healed and I did not look for any more adventures. I decided not to sell my horse, I kept her, and I was able to find work around town for my horse and wagon. Belka presented us with another calf, but we sold it. We began to receive mail from my brothers and sisters in America again, asking if we were willing now to come. The answer was still no as my father would not hear of it. He said: "After I die you can do what you want."

On the twenty-seventh day of August 1919, Father was sitting at the table in the living room. As usual he was praying and studying the Talmud. I was home alone. Mother and Frumke were out shopping at the market. It was a little before two in the afternoon . . .

Lazar was in the kitchen finishing his lunch. He had been out since early that morning bringing a load of flour from the mill to the baker and had come home about an hour before, famished. He didn't want to disturb his father, so he ate alone in the kitchen. As he finished the last of his milk and babka, he was thinking about what still had to be done before the High Holidays, to fix the roof on the barn, weather-strip the windows, stock up on firewood, load up on hay for the animals, bring in the potatoes, there was a lot to do. Rosh Hashanah was less than a month away and Lazar always tried to have as much done as possible for the winter before Rosh Hashanah, because nothing would get done between Rosh Hashanah and Yom Kippur, and after Yom Kippur the cold weather would set in. Funny the way the Day of Atonement always seemed to be the dividing line between warm weather and cold, even though it came at different times on the calendar each year. I wonder if there is some connection, Lazar thought, I must remember to ask Father how the date came to be set originally.

But not now because Father was studying the Talmud. Lazar thought about his father in the other room, poring over his books day in and day out. He had no understanding of his father's scholarly preoccupation with religious study but it was not something he questioned. Father was a scholar. It had been going on for as long as Lazar could remember, and it was as much a matter of course for his father to study as it was for him to work.

Still, it would be nice if Father wasn't always studying, if sometimes we could just go for walks or something or maybe even go fishing the way Boris does with his father. Even if we didn't catch anything, that would be nice. And if I didn't always have to be thinking about working and making money, that would be nice too, Lazar thought. There wasn't much time for fun in his life.

Girls, for instance. Chanka, for instance. He hadn't seen Chanka in a long time and he missed her. He dreamed of Chanka again last night and had another wet dream. That was something else he didn't understand about, wet dreams. Was that normal? Could he get sick from having too many? Or from playing with himself at night? Frumke said he shouldn't do it, but what did she know, she was a girl. Maybe he would try to get over to see Chanka soon and have some loving, that would be better than dreaming about her at night, dreaming about kissing and hugging and touching her breasts and . . .

What's the matter with me, he thought, there's plenty of

*work for me to do and all I can think about is fooling
around with Chanka? I'd better clean up here and get busy
with that roof on the barn, all thinking about Chanka is
going to get me is more cramps.*

*As Lazar was thinking all this he heard the chair scrape
the floor in the living room as it was pushed back from the
table. He heard his father get up and walk slowly toward
the bedroom. He must be tired, Lazar thought, and he's going in to lie down. Lazar picked up his dishes and started
toward the sink with them when he heard a heavy thud,
something falling to the floor in the bedroom, and instantly
the sound registered a picture without having to be put
into words. Lazar put the dishes down and ran to the bedroom.*

*His father was stretched out on the floor on his back, his
face white as a sheet, his eyes fluttering open and staring
up in confusion, as though he didn't know where he was.
He made an attempt to prop himself up on one elbow but
he was having a difficult time of it. Lazar bent over his father, pulled him to the bureau and helped him to sit up so
that his back was leaning against the bureau.*

*"Tate, Tate, was hat getroffen mit der?" he asked in Yid-
dish.*

*His father responded weakly that he didn't know what
had happened, he had simply blacked out and fallen
down. He asked Lazar to help him into bed. His father's
bed was across the room, his mother's bed was close at
hand, so Lazar helped his father up and into his mother's
bed. The color was not returning to his father's face and he
still appeared weak and confused. He was breathing in
rapid shallow breaths. Lazar didn't know what he should
do. Should he run for Dr. Weiner or should he stay with
his father? He decided to stay. Mother would be home soon
and she would know what to do. And just as he said that to
himself, he heard his mother and sister returning.*

He rushed to the front door, swung it open and yelled: "Mother, come quick, Father fainted and he doesn't look good and I don't know what to do!" His mother handed him the bag of groceries and hurried into the bedroom. He heard her asking: "Dovid, how do you feel?" but he couldn't hear his father's reply. His mother came back out.

"Frumke, run for the doctor and be quick. Tell him it's an emergency. Lazar, you go stay with your father. I'll make some tea." She rolled up her sleeves and went into the kitchen. Frumke left immediately for the doctor. Lazar went into the bedroom.

"It's all right, Father, I'll stay with you. Frumke went to get Dr. Weiner and Mother's making some tea. Are you feeling a little better? Does anything hurt? Is there anything I can do for you?"

"No, I'm fine, nothing hurts, thank you. Tell me about what you've been doing, Layshka."

Lazar told him about the trip to the mill, about his various work projects getting ready for the winter, all the time his father was lying there with his eyes closed, nodding his head and smiling weakly, and Lazar was practically on the verge of tears but he managed to smile back at his father and pretend he was relaxed. Finally, his father held up a hand and asked Lazar if he would help him to his own bed. Lazar supported him across the room. He was surprisingly small and frail, and the effort to get into his own bed exhausted him. His breathing was labored.

Frumke returned with Dr. Weiner. The doctor lived nearby and had his office in his house. He always kept his horse and carriage hitched out front and ready for emergencies, so he had driven right over with Frumke. Dr. Weiner went into the bedroom to examine Lazar's father. Lazar and Frumke sat together in the living room, their mother was in the kitchen. Ten minutes later Dr. Weiner came out of the bedroom and went into the kitchen to talk with their mother. They couldn't hear what was being said. Then Dr. Weiner left. Their mother stood at the door watching Dr. Weiner drive away.

"Is Father going to be all right, Mother?" asked Frumke.

"He'll be fine," she answered, but she had a distant look in her eyes which neither of them had ever seen before. "Why don't you go feed the animals, Layshka, and Frumke, you can help me with dinner."

Lazar started to protest that the animals had been fed in the morning the way they always were, but he thought better of it and went outside anyway. For the next two hours Lazar sat in the barn with Belka and Rosetka and the mare, and he prayed. Somehow he knew what was coming. The walks he had been thinking about earlier, fishing together in the river, it wasn't going to happen. Tears filled his eyes as he sat and waited.

It was growing dark. Lazar went back to the house. He looked at the clock. It was not quite six. His mother handed him a glass of warm milk and told him to take it in to his father. As he tiptoed into the room, his father opened his eyes and smiled weakly. One hand lifted slightly off the bed and dropped down again. Lazar sat on the edge of the bed, put his right arm behind his father's back and helped him to sit up in order to drink the milk. Neither of them spoke.

His father seemed much weaker. Lazar held the glass of milk in his left hand and supported his father with his right. He brought the glass to his father's lips. His father took two small sips of milk. Then he closed his eyes, turned his head slightly to the side, and died. The last sip of warm milk trickled slowly from the corner of his mouth and formed tiny white droplets on his gray beard. Lazar sat there, stunned, the glass of milk in one hand, his father's lifeless body in the other, and he stared at his father in disbelief.

"Father! Father! Open your eyes! Don't die, Father, please don't die. I don't want you to die! Open your eyes!"

He was screaming. His mother and Frumke came running in. Frumke screamed once and started crying. His mother took his father by his shoulders and shook him gently. No response. She put her head to his chest and listened. Nothing. She forced one eyelid open with two fingers, held it open for a moment as the eye stared straight ahead without blinking, then she closed it, told Lazar to let him go and get up, gently laid her husband down on the bed, sighed, stood up and walked slowly out of the room, her head bowed, her arms loosely at her sides.

At the doorway, she stopped, turned her head, and said, "Come, children."

. . . He died in a very peaceful way. Mother knew that it was going to happen because the doctor said it was only a matter of time, but she didn't know it was going to happen that soon. She never forgave herself for not being at his bedside when he died.

Since he died after sundown, the funeral could not take place until the next day. That meant he had to lie on the floor on a few pieces of straw all night, which was the Orthodox custom. We notified the *Hevrah Kaddisha*, a few men from the synagogue who were dedicated to taking care of all funeral arrangements. They came and took him off his bed and placed him on the floor. Two men sat and prayed all night. I sat alongside my father the whole night, praying and crying.

In the morning several men came and prepared him for his burial. They washed his body and put him in shrouds. Then they put on him his tallith and tefillin and they placed his yarmulke on his head. They put him on a table and covered him with a black cloth and they carried him to the cemetery. We all stood there as they lowered him into his grave and put him on the ground. Then they put three

184

boards over him and shoveled the dirt back in until the grave was filled. I recited the Kaddish.

After the funeral we sat shiva for seven days and observed sheloshim for thirty days which was the Orthodox custom. I went to synagogue three times a day, at shaharith (morning services), minhah (afternoon) and maariv (evening), to pray and to recite the Kaddish. I did this for a whole year and I never missed a day . . .

To Lazar, religion was not something you thought about, it was something you did. What he knew, he had been taught, by his father and by the Rabbi, the same things repeated over and over until he knew them by heart. Much of it he did not understand, he was, after all, not a religious scholar like his father, but he questioned none of it. It was enough that his father said it was so. He never asked why.

But when he did it, when he prayed like this in synagogue, when he laid tefillin, the two black leather boxes containing four portions of the Pentateuch on parchment and bound by leather straps to his left arm and his forehead, when he wore the tallith and yarmulke his father had given him at his bar mitzvah, and when he davened with the minyan as he was doing this morning, he just felt so good inside, as if he . . . belonged, and it made him feel very proud.

He was Eleazar Ben-David . . . Lazar, son of Dovid Unovitch, a descendent of the ancient tribe of Levi, second in responsibility only to the Cohens, the priests, and charged by Moses to assist the Cohens in the Tabernacle and to instruct the people in the Torah, the book of laws . . . Eleazar Ben-David who now recited the mourner's Kaddish as he had every morning, afternoon, and evening for the past year in memory of his dear departed father:

185

Yisgadal v'yiskadash sh'may rabo,
B'olmo dee v'ro hirusay, v'yamleeh malhusay,
B'hayayhōn uvyōmayhōn, uvhayay d'hol bays yisroayl,
Baagolo uviz'man koreev, v'imru omayn.
V'hay sh'may rabo m'vorah, l'olam ulolmay olmayo.
Visborah v'yishtabah, v'yispoar v'yisrōmam,
V'yisnasay v'yishadar, v'yisaleh, v'yishalal
*   sh'may d'kudsho b'rih hu;*
L'aylo min kol birhoso v'sheeroso,
Tushb'hoso v'nehehmoso, daameeron b'olmo,
V'imru omayn.

Y'hay sh'lomo rabo min sh'mayo,
V'hayeem olaynu v'al kol yisroayl v'imru omayn.
May there be great peace from heaven and life for us
*   and*
all Israel. And let us say Amen.

Ōse sholōm bimromōv hu yaase sholōm
Olaynu v'al kol yisroayl v'imru omayn.
May the One who makes peace in the heavens make
*   peace*
for us and for all of Israel. And let us say Amen.

The unveiling of the gravestone took place at the ceme-
tery on 27 August 1920, one year following his father's
death. It had been a long, hard year and they had all
missed him very much, but the year was over. They were
free to leave at last. Lazar's older brother Benel had mar-
ried a woman from Libova, Poland. Her brother was a
vice-president of Cunard Lines and through him, Lazar's
brothers and sisters had succeeded in making arrange-
ments for first-class passage at a greatly reduced price for
Lazar, Frumke, and their mother. Their papers and tickets
had arrived. All that remained was to obtain passports and
exit papers and to arrange to sell the house and building,
the livestock, and whatever possessions they could not take
along on the trip.
*   Lazar was going to America.*

Chapter Nine

1. ✤

"I just got a tip that the Poles are going to arrest Lazar this afternoon. I came over as soon as I heard."

It was Ivan the policeman. Ivan had been a good friend of the family for many years and often dropped by for a cup of tea while making his rounds, especially when it was as cold out as it was today. It was the end of September but winter was already in the air. It would be a short fall this year.

But it wasn't cold weather that brought Ivan today, nor even the thick slice of fresh-baked black bread Lazar's mother was holding out to him, steam rising from the still-warm bread and the freshly churned sweet butter she had spread thickly on it already melting, though it was indeed a delicacy Ivan could never refuse, all one hundred and ten kilos of him. No, what brought Ivan today was concern for Lazar and he was flushed and out of breath after hurrying from the police station to warn his friends.

He accepted the bread with an appreciative nod, though, and took a huge bite of it as Lazar jumped up from his chair and shouted, "Arrested! What did I do?"

Ivan frowned, started to answer, couldn't with half a

187

slice of bread and butter in his mouth, chewed rapidly, holding up his hand for Lazar to wait, swallowed hard but too soon, gagged, coughed and finally managed to gain enough control of himself to answer.

"Remember two years ago you were in the mounted police for the Bolsheviks and brought all those women in for questioning about three men in the Polish Underground? One of those men was an important agent for all of Belorussia. His daughter was one of the women and she claims she was raped, and he's pressing charges. Your old captain was transferred to Petrograd or somewhere, and two of the boys went into the Red Army, but they've been looking for the other three of you.

"The Poles made an inquiry to my chief yesterday and this morning I overheard him identify you as one of the three, Lazar. He has notified the Polish authorities and they plan to make the arrest this afternoon. They mean to make an example of you."

"Oh my god!" cried Lazar's mother, her eyes wide, her hand flying to her mouth. "What can we do?"

Frumke was frightened and started to cry. She put her arms around Lazar protectively. Lazar couldn't believe it was happening. Police coming to arrest him? Ivan looked from one to the other. He was concerned. He wanted to help. He knew they were getting ready to leave for America, everyone in the neighborhood knew it, and he also knew that Lazar had never done anyone any harm.

"You will have to hide until you are ready to leave town," Ivan said. "Do you know anyone who might have room for you? I would do it if I could, even though it would be very dangerous, but I don't have anywhere to hide you."

"What about next door?" suggested Lazar's mother.

"No good," Ivan replied. "It's too close, they're sure to look there."

"Yes, but they're Polish," Lazar said, "and the Poles

would never bother them, not after those Polish soldiers killed their son. I could hide in their barn!"

Ivan changed his mind. Lazar was right, it would be an excellent place to hide. Frumke ran next door to find out if it would be all right. She returned a few minutes later, saying their neighbors had agreed immediately. After the way Lazar had tried to save their son's life that day, they would do anything to help him.

Quickly the two women gathered blankets and food as Lazar threw together some extra clothing. They tied it all into a big bundle. Ivan went out first to make sure the way was clear. Lazar kissed his mother and sister, gathered the bundle into both arms, and ran as fast as he could to the neighbor's barn, shouting to Ivan as he passed him: Thank you, Ivan! God bless you, Ivan! I'll see you in America! and he didn't stop running until he reached the barn, climbed up the ladder into the hayloft and flung himself down on the sweet-smelling mound of yellow hay.

Was there no end to his troubles? It was something that Lazar thought a lot about for the five weeks he lived in his neighbor's hayloft. There was nothing else to do most of the time. The weather remained cold, but Lazar had tunneled himself a sort of cave in the hay, and bundled in the blankets he was pretty warm, actually. No complaints there. Occasionally the farmer would call him into the house for a hot meal, sending his grandchildren outside to keep watch while Lazar ate. He was a good friend, the farmer.

At night Lazar would climb down from the hayloft and walk around a bit to get some exercise, but he was afraid to do it for very long for fear he would be spotted even in the dark. Every two or three nights Frumke would sneak over with more food and a change of clothes and she would tell Lazar the news. Polish police had come to the house several times, looking for him. A man dressed in plain clothes was with them, the girl's father, probably. Once, they had even come at night and searched the entire house and barn, but thank god they had not bothered Mother or her. They had found nothing and left.

After the first week or so the Polish police stopped coming around, but Lazar was taking no chances. He would stay in the hayloft until they were ready to leave. Frumke reported that their mother had been unable to find a buyer for the house or the apartments. Times were hard and nobody had any money. She did manage to sell the mare and the wagon but not the cow. Belka would be given to the neighbor for hiding Lazar. Rosetka too. As for the house and apartments, she had decided to give them to Uncle Schmuel who would try to sell them later if he could and would send them the money if he was successful. If not, what could they do? It was either give the place to Uncle Schmuel or don't go to America. They already had the tickets from his brother Benel, a complete package deal including trains, hotels, and steamships. The passports were due in a day or two. Not going was just about out of the question.

"Mother says to be ready. When the passports arrive, we will take the night train to Warsaw. We're all packed. Uncle Schmuel will drive us to the station. You're supposed to meet us at the train. I'm to tell you which car and which compartment as soon as it's arranged. Don't worry, Lazar," Frumke said, flashing a dimpled smile, "we're going to America, all three of us. Just be ready."

Ready? Oh, he was ready, all right, he had been ready a long time, hanging around this damn hayloft for five weeks with nothing to do but spend all night banging his stick to scare the mice away, god how he hated mice! and all day worrying about whether the Poles would finally decide to search this barn for him after all.

What had he ever done to deserve this? He tried to explain to those women that day that he meant them no harm, that he was only obeying his Captain's orders to guard them, that he had only joined the mounted police in the first place so he could avoid the draft and make some money for his family. He never thought he was going to have to arrest somebody. And he had been scared to death when his Captain raped that girl! He himself had been raped once and he knew how terrible it could be, so terrible he couldn't bear to think about it even now.

Somehow things always seemed to go bad for him. It wasn't fair. All he had ever done was work hard and try to be good, and yet somehow he always ended up in trouble for something he didn't do. Five weeks hiding in a hayloft because someone wanted an example made and he was the only one around. Five weeks in a hayloft afraid of his own shadow and waiting to go to America. What if there was more trouble waiting for him there? He didn't even speak English. How would he get work? How would he support the three of them without a horse and wagon, without any land, without any money?

Maybe it was wrong to go to America. Maybe he was meant to stay here. The house, the barn, the brick building his mother and father had worked so hard to build and take care of, maybe it was better for him to stay here and take care of the property, instead of giving it away to Uncle Schmuel. And what about Chanka? She was the only girl he had ever loved, the only girl he had ever thought of marrying. He would never see her again! Nor Belka, Rosetka, the mare! How could he leave them all?

But this was foolish! How could he stay, the Poles would arrest him sooner or later, he couldn't stay up here in the hayloft forever. Oh, it was all so confusing! But what could he do about it anyway? God decided everything and God never asked Lazar what he thought. There was nothing he could do about it, it was all in God's hands. What's bershert is bershert. If God wants him to go to America, he will go to America; if God wants the Poles to catch him, he will be caught. That's the way Lazar thought, and thinking that way made Lazar feel terrible, and he cried himself to sleep every night for five weeks.

2. ﬡ

"We leave tomorrow night. The passports came today and Mother went to the train station and made reservations. We have a compartment all to ourselves on the night train to Warsaw. Oh, Lazar, isn't it exciting? We're going to America!"

Frumke's words last night still rang in his ears. They were finally leaving! Boris and Moishe and some of his other friends had come by the house yesterday to say good-bye. Friends of the family had been dropping in all week to say good-bye to his mother, everybody laughing and crying at the same time and saying how happy they were for her to be rejoining her other children after so many years, but how much they were going to miss her and Frumke and Lazar.

So many people knew they were leaving, Lazar was certain the Polish police must know it by now too, how could they not? Boris told Frumke that the police had questioned both him and Moishe about his whereabouts. The Poles were still after him. He was frightened and on edge, jumping at the slightest sound. Would they grab him as he left here, or at the station, or on the train? Lazar had the awful feeling he was going to be caught at the last minute, that something would happen to prevent him from leaving for America.

The day was interminable. He had hardly slept all night. He glanced at the bag of fruit and cold chicken

Frumke had brought him and realized he should eat some-thing, but he rejected the idea. He was too nervous to eat. Rosetka was with him. Frumke had brought her so that they could be together his last night. And Belka had been in a stall below, the farmer having brought her over yes-terday too. She was at pasture with the other cows now. Just as well.

Last night had been a reunion, like the good old days when he used to sit in the barn with Belka and Rosetka and talk to them about how the three of them would be to-gether always. Funny how things had worked out. He tried to explain it to them last night, how sometimes a man had to do things differently from the way he planned as a boy, how he had to go away now but they would have a good home here and he would always remember them and they would always be friends.

It was hard to leave them and his other friends, but La-zar had faced hard things before, plenty of them. He was a man now, after all, not a boy anymore, and it would not do to cry. The important thing was not to be caught by the police and he prayed for God to help him. Late in the afternoon the farmer came to say good-bye. He stood in the hayloft with Lazar and wished him good luck in America and not to worry about his animals, they would be well cared for. Then he embraced Lazar, kissed him on both cheeks, and went back down the ladder with Rosetka tucked under one arm so she wouldn't try to follow Lazar when he left.

The sun was down and it was almost time to leave. Lazar took off his old clothes, folded them into a neat pile, and put on his good suit. He moved slowly, as though in a dream. Perhaps it was a dream, it all seemed so unreal. But was it a good dream or a bad one? Lazar wondered. Well, he would know soon enough. It was time to go. Lazar took a deep breath and started down the ladder.

Once outside the barn, he paused for a moment to listen, then began to make his way through the fields. It was the long way to the station but it was safer. He couldn't chance using the streets. As he got closer to the station, he slowed and moved more cautiously. He had planned the route carefully the night before. Around the prison, behind the mill, along the back road to the army post, across the far end of the market, and finally to the warehouse across from the station.

He stood in the shadows alongside the warehouse, watching the platform. He could see the big clock outside the ticket office. Twenty-five minutes to go. The train was in the station and waiting, steam rising from beneath the locomotive. It must have gotten here early, he thought. The platform was empty except for the engineer and the conductor talking to each other next to the engine, and a man and woman standing with a soldier toward the rear of the train.

As Lazar watched, his uncle's wagon came down the street and stopped next to the platform. Uncle Schmuel got down first and then helped his mother and sister. They stood by the wagon for a moment, looking around for Lazar, and Lazar almost yelled across to them, but just then he spotted two policemen walking slowly along the sidewalk near the cab stand, heading in his direction.

He held his breath. What should he do? He watched them, terrified, as they continued toward him, and he was just about to turn and run when they suddenly veered across the street and headed for the station platform. Oh god, they must be looking for him!

Uncle Schmuel unloaded the wagon. Three large wicker suitcases and a huge cream-colored sack. Frumke had told him about the sack, that was going to be for him to carry, that and one suitcase but it was the sack that he would have to guard with his life. It contained two large quilts and four big pillows, all of them filled with goose down, plus the brass samovar and the brass shtasel Mother used to grind spices. The brass pieces had belonged to her grandmother and the down quilts and pillows had been the products of many winters' work. Frumke said Mother had insisted they go no matter how big the sack was; if the sack didn't go, she didn't go!

Lazar continued to watch as they carried the luggage to the third car behind the locomotive, Uncle Schmuel struggling to get the sack through the car door. He saw them move through the car and enter a compartment on the platform side of the train. Uncle Schmuel put the sack down on a seat and kissed the women good-bye. He made his way back through the car, got off, climbed into his wagon, waved, and drove away. Lazar could see his mother and sister peering anxiously through the window, watching for him.

The two policemen were talking to the engineer and the conductor. He looked at the clock. Ten minutes. What should he do? Wait or take a chance? What if they were waiting for him? Sweat ran down his temples. He shivered. He'd better wait.

The engineer climbed back into the cabin of the locomotive. The young soldier embraced his mother and father and boarded the train. The couple turned and walked away down the street. Five minutes. Oh god, hurry up, it's almost time!

The conductor pulled out his pocket watch, looked at it, glanced over at the station clock and back at his watch, wound it and put it away.

Three minutes! The conductor said good-bye to the policemen and started walking toward the middle of the train. Alll aboard!

The policemen walked slowly toward the front of the platform.

Mother and Frumke were talking to each other, their lips moving rapidly and with great agitation. Mother was shaking her head and gathering up the suitcases.

Two minutes! The policemen and the conductor were five cars apart.

It was now or never. Lazar made a mad dash across the street, jumped onto the platform and raced toward the third car. Mother and Frumke spotted him and waved frantically. The engineer blew two short blasts on the train whistle. Lazar grabbed the handrail, pulled himself up into the car, ran down the passageway, ducked into the compartment with his mother and Frumke, and flung himself down on the seat next to the sack, exhausted, just as the train began to move slowly forward.

His mother was thanking God. Frumke had her arms around his neck, laughing hysterically. Lazar looked out the window. The two policemen were crossing the street toward the cab stand, continuing their rounds. They hadn't seen him. The train gathered speed as the engineer let out one long blast on the whistle. The policemen were growing smaller and smaller and finally disappeared altogether, along with the cab stand, the station, and Volkovysk.

Notes on Process

1. Lazar's story requires no explanation. It is what it is, a simple story of the adventures of a boy growing up in Russia during a tumultuous period of history, with additional interest, perhaps, in knowing that the story has been based on recollective notes done by Lazar some sixty years later and has been written by his son. What complicates the matter is the issue of time travel, the process by which I have been able to "become" Lazar in order to experience for myself these adventures which have been only thinly sketched in my father's notes.

I can no more easily explain *how* I do this than you can explain how you dream. I just do it and I don't question afterward whether it "actually" happened or whether it was "real." My father's notes serve as cues. I use no formal induction procedure. There is, however, a very definite mind-set: I allow myself to be in an open and highly suggestible state, relaxed, alone and quiet. Undistracted, or it doesn't happen.

Beyond that, the nearest thing to an explanation is contained in these notes which I kept sporadically while writing the book. I do not pass this off as a scientific experiment, far from it. As Arthur Koestler has pointed out:

Paranormal events, whether produced in the laboratory or spontaneously, are unpredictable, capricious and relatively rare. This is one of the reasons why skeptics feel justified in rejecting the results of some forty years of vigorously controlled laboratory experiments in ESP and PK [psychokinesis] in spite of the massive statistical evidence which, in any other field of research, would be considered as sufficient proof for the reality of the phenomena.

But the criterion of repeatability applies only when the experimental conditions are essentially the same as in the original experiment; and with sensitive human subjects the conditions are never quite the same in terms of mood, receptivity, or emotional rapport between subject and experimenter. Besides, ESP phenomena nearly always involve unconscious processes beyond voluntary control.[1]

2. I was explaining to my brother, or rather trying to, what it was that I was attempting to do with our father's notes and how, in order to accomplish that, I was time-traveling to Volkovysk. He didn't get it. He didn't want to get it, the whole idea was contrary to his belief system.

"Look," I said, "let's just say then that I am using my imagination and that imagination is a form of time travel."

"Oh," he responded, "that's different. If you're telling me that 'time travel' is imagination, I can accept that."

I gave up. We believe what we want to believe.

3. When I began several years ago to research autohypnosis as a technique for age regression,* I first read everything I could on the subject and then received practical instruction from Dr. Fred Frankel, then President of the International Society of Clinical and Experimental Hypnosis. As a result, and with considerable practice, I was able to elicit in myself nearly every known hypnotic phenomenon, except that I was still unable to age-regress. To breach the impasse I sought the help of Theodore X. Barber, an international authority on hypnosis, at this writing Director of Special Projects of the Massachusetts Department of Mental Health at Cushing Hospital in Framingham, Massachusetts.

Barber is unique in the field; among other things, he doesn't believe there is such a thing as hypnosis. "Anything you can do in a trance," he told me, "you can do while you're wide awake, pro-

*See *my*, "The Door in the Wall," *Human Behavior*, June–July–August 1978.

vided you *think with* or *imagine with* the idea." And the key to age regression, I learned from Barber, is to suspend criticality.

It took me almost six months to learn *how* to do that, to unlearn reason; and then I was able to age-regress to my own childhood, using various cues, principally physical locations and photographs, to assist me in the process. I accepted everything that I experienced as happening literally but at another level of reality which I came to know as *fourth dimensional,* that is, where time and space are not separate entities but form a continuum in which past, present, and future coexist simultaneously, or, put another way, do not exist at all but are instead replaced by a sort of tenseless Now.

The more I practiced the easier it became, and eventually I reached the conclusion that with even more practice I ought to be able to go anywhere I wished on that continuum. It was at that point that I began to work with my father's notes. Age-regressing to *his* boyhood seemed merely an extension of age-regressing to my own. However, I soon discovered there were substantial differences. These periodically confused and troubled me to such an extent that, Barber notwithstanding, I needed clarification, and validation, outside of my own experiences. I found both in quantum physics.

4. [Following the scene in the schoolyard in Chapter One in which Lazar is picked on by four older Russian boys and then defended by the Polish boy, Gregori.] Strange, that scene in the schoolyard, I am still feeling it. The scene was real, as real as sitting here on the boat and writing about it is to me now, and yet I was not always sure that it was his life I was in. I had a similar experience in my own life. There are such parallels in our lives, no, more than that, synchronicities for which I have no explanation. We are very much alike, my father and I.

In the schoolyard, I *was* him. I was also me. But at times there was no separation at all and I sensed that our lives and our experiences are interchangeable. It was no longer his life or my life then, it was *our* life, an incident happening to both of us as one. Two different pasts somehow merged into one *tenseless* present. Where? How?

Is there perhaps already a sort of cosmic recombinant DNA program in effect? Is there a time beyond space-time where all times merge? Are experiences like this one a glimpse of what lies beyond the edge? Lately there are times when I feel connected to everything and everyone, when I actually experience the flow of something, whatever it is, that causes me however fleetingly to know the interchangeability of all things as a universal reality, what the new physicists call the "Quantum Inseparability Principle."

But I can't sustain the feeling, no matter how hard I try. I find myself almost instantly back in my three-dimensional reality, struggling to understand intellectually what I have just experienced intuitively. And once again I am faced with the impossibility of proving and communicating the experience of a temporal symmetry that appears to defy the language and the law of a physical universe.

Two days later I was with Jacob Sarfatti, a quantum physicist and former research assistant to British physicist David Bohm. We sat at an outside table at the Savoy-Tivoli in San Francisco's North Beach, one of Jack's "offices," and I reviewed my thoughts following the schoolyard scene.

"Oh, sure," said Sarfatti, "that's related to QUIP, the Quantum Inseparability Principle." And my reference to the possibility of a time beyond space-time where all times merge, he explained, could be found in David Bohm's theory of the Implicate Order. These are the notations Sarfatti made for me on sheets of blank computer-readout paper while lecturing to me on quantum physics, 21 September 1978:

5. [Chapter Four. German soldiers now occupy Volkovysk. I am approaching the rape scene with great trepidation. For the last three weeks it has been increasingly on my mind. I am filled with anxiety, nervous, apprehensive, not sleeping well. I know it is coming. I know that I will have to be Lazar in that scene, go through it myself. I am intimidated by that knowledge, and yet . . .]

I am living in two different lives.

One, I am here on the boat. I see no one and I go nowhere. I have totally immersed myself in being alone and writing my father's story. It is a lonely and solitary life. I am worried that the book is moving too slowly. Sometimes I also worry that it may not

QUANTUM PHYSICS!

AXIOM: UNDER CERTAIN CONDITIONS IT IS POSSIBLE TO TRANSMIT OR RECEIVE MESSAGES WITHOUT INTERMEDIARY SIGNALS. → HYPOTHESIS CONSCIOUSNESS "IS" FASTER-THAN-LIGHT MESSAGES WITHOUT SIGNALS ← TO-BE DEVELOPED.

QUANTUM MECHANICS OPERATES ON A LEVEL OF REALITY, WHICH IS BEYOND SPACE-TIME IN WHICH "CAUSE—EFFECT" (PRINCIPLE OF LOCAL CAUSES BREAKS DOWN).

"QUP"

BELL'S THEOREM

H. P. STAPP LBL "QM" DESTROYS FUNDAMENTAL STATUS OF SPACE-TIME SEPARATIONS. QM DESTROYS THE DISTINCTION BETWEEN PRIMARY & SECONDARY QUALITIES

BOHM SAYS THERE ARE TWO KINDS OF "TIME"

"EINSTEIN—ROSEN—PODOLSKY EFFECT OR "PARADOX" OF 1935.

"QUANTUM INSEPARABILITY"

BOHM: "IMPLICATE" ORDER. HOLOGRAPHICALLY ENFOLDED WITHIN EXPLICATE ORDER OF SPACE-TIME.

RELATES TO MEMORY—PRIBRAM

OUTER (EXPLICATE) TIME ⌐ MEASURED WITH PHYSICIST'S CLOCKS

INNER (IMPLICATE) "TIME" ⌐ (DUNNE EXPERIMENT IN TIME. JUNGIAN "SYNCHRONICITY" ACAUSAL MEANINGFUL COINCIDENCE.

QUANTUM PRINCIPLE.

"I AM THE ALPHA, AND THE OMEGA, THAT WHICH WAS, AND WHICH IS, AND WHICH IS TO COME." = QUP

ANALOGOUS TO HOLOGRAPHIC PLATE

ONE "MOMENT" OF INNER TIME IS A SUPERPOSITION OF ALL MOMENTS OF "OUTER" TIME — AND VICE VERSA ⟶ "HOLOGRAM".

PARELLELS → JESUS.

EXPLICATE

COKE

COMETH NOT WITH OBSERVATION, LO, NEITHER HERE NOR THERE ← QUP —NON LOCATION THE TEMPLE OF GOD IS WITHIN YOU. CONSCIOUSNESS IS THE IMPLICATE ORDER OF QUANTUM MECHANICS BEYOND SPACE-TIME.

be going well, but who is there to say? It is a very great trust he has placed in me.

Two, I am here in Volkovysk, happy. This is my hometown, the house, the barn, the streets and shops, the market. And I am surrounded by people, the family, the animals, Joe, Chanka, these are mine also and I feel very close to them. As for Lazar, I do not understand our relationship. I only know that I love him and that I am as comfortable with him as I am with myself.

It is a strange life. I always know what is to come, and yet I am no less conscious of my free will to affect what takes place. No one I tell this to understands, so I have stopped telling it. Even knowing the hardships to come, and the limitations, I am still excited by each new adventure, and in some way which I do not yet comprehend, I am fulfilled by it. So much so that when one of them ends, I am annoyed as though I have been awakened from a pleasureful dream, which is strange in itself because I am both the awakened and the awakener.

My usual pleasure at watching the size of a manuscript grow is being overshadowed by anxiety at the diminution of the notes yet to be lived. I am worried that the book is moving too quickly. More than one hundred and fifty pages of his notes have been used up already and there are not that many more still to be added.

This book will end when he goes to America, but I have asked him to continue the notes at least until my conception; and I am now watching both ends of this life at the same time. While I am in Volkovysk in the middle of a war just begun, he is already in America getting married. The latest batch of notes are of his wedding night in Pittsburgh. I told him he need proceed no further than my conception, but as that time is getting closer I am growing apprehensive. It is as though I anticipate death rather than birth. Yes, but whose?

The line was drawn a long time ago. All I can do is follow it. What is to come in one life has already happened in the other. There is my father in Florida now and my father in Pittsburgh then; and there is me on the boat now and Lazar in Volkovysk then. But if then is both now and yet to be for me, what is now if not the same for someone else?

6. [Chapter Five. Something has been nagging at me for some time. I have been reading *Uri*,[2] in which Puharich describes Uri

Geller's powers as being transmitted to him by an extraterrestrial solid-state entity known as "The Nine." The Nine communicates with Puharich and Geller by means of various solid-state receivers, telephones, tape recorders, television sets. This might mean that these messages are coming from the past since they would have had to take the time required for radio waves to travel to earth from another star system.

However, Puharich describes the powers as being transmitted directly to Geller, implying a faster-than-light (FTL) communication system, in other words telepathy, in which case The Nine could be communicating either from the present or even more likely from the future. Moreover, Geller has no control over the receipt of these messages or powers and what he had assumed to be his own innate extrasensory abilities are, according to both Puharich and Geller, at least partially endowed in him by an entity or entities for their own purposes, quite possibly from the future; and, even after they made themselves known to Geller, this continues often without Geller's conscious knowledge or approval.

A similar situation is described in *Seth Speaks*,[3] one of several books written by Jane Roberts from material provided by a personality calling himself "Seth" who speaks through her while she is in a trance state. At one point Seth explains that "he" has been preparing Jane Roberts for many years, without her knowledge, for the time (now) when "he" will be able to speak through her. I am both intrigued and frightened by the idea of unconscious influence in the form of telepathic communication from another time frame, a sort of metaphysical mind control. The implications are awesome!]

Do I have the right to be doing this?

What are my moral and ethical responsibilities, moving in and out of Lazar this way? My father's tacit approval is hardly sufficient, nor valid, since it may not even be his to grant. What rights does even he have where Lazar the boy is concerned? Lazar exists independently from the person he will eventually become, exists in that time frame to which we refer temporally as "past." And the events about which my father and I write with historicity are still occurring in that time frame.

When I enter and become Lazar, I do so without his knowledge or consent. I invade his privacy. Regardless of my good intentions there are moral and ethical considerations involved when invading someone's privacy, even though the invasion is metaphysical. Does Lazar not have rights in such a matter? How are these rights to be protected? Do I in turn have rights protecting me from an invasion of privacy from the future? How to enforce these rights when there are no controls? And what does that say about free will and self-determination, about the inviolability of Self?

Until now my belief was that whatever my effect on Lazar's life, it is only a subtle one since I cannot alter his history as I know it from my father's notes. So I believed. *But, what if events in Lazar's life were actually determined in part by what I am doing now!* There is a way to test the thesis, but do I dare? If I am wrong there is no harm done; if I am right I not only tamper with Lazar's history, I risk affecting my own existence!

7. *Both Ayer and Russell* [A. J. Ayer, Bertrand Russell] *seem to have claimed that it is logically possible that men should affect the past. Both have urged that it is only the fact that we know so much about the past that makes us think that we cannot affect it. But, they claim, our relatively greater knowledge of the past than the future is a contingent matter. Hence in a world where we knew relatively little about the past, it would be sensible for us to try and influence it. Thus Ayer in* The Problem Of Knowledge *couched his discussion of the question as follows: "The reason then why we do not allow ourselves to conceive of our actions as affecting past events is, I suggest, not merely that the earlier events already exist, but that they are for the most part, already known to exist. Since the same does not apply to the future, we come to think of our action as essentially forward moving."—* Richard Swinburne[4]

You're stuck with a grotesque and absurd illusion ... the idea of time as an ever-rolling stream. There's one thing certain in this business: the idea of time as a steady progression from past to future is wrong. I know very well we feel this way about it subjectively. But we're the victim of a confidence trick."—Sir Fred Hoyle, astronomer[5]

8. [Chapter Six. Lazar's job on the farm has ended as a result of the injury to his foot. It seems a good time to take a break. My father is anxious to hear of the progress of the book. I am still con-

cerned about invading Lazar's privacy and about the possibility of influencing his life from the future (my present). I decide to fly to Florida to review with him what has been written thus far, but more importantly (to me) to probe his memory for any evidence that Lazar might somehow have become aware of "outside" influence on his life.]

Winter came while I was away. All the warm sounds are gone. A cold southerly has been blowing a symphony of clanging halyards for three days, freezing the sun and sending whitecaps sweeping through the nearly deserted harbor. The gulls circle silently now, their search for food no longer a game. No day sailors, no crusts of bread and apple peels; no fishermen, no fish heads. In winter there is less to sing about.

It was hot and humid in Florida, more like summer than winter. Winter here, summer there, spring in Volkovysk. These seasonal shifts upset my rhythm. I questioned my father carefully. There was little he could add to his notes. When I asked about Lazar I referred to him in the third person, but when my father answered he used the first person. I found that confusing. (If this is such a simple story, why am I making it so complex?)

I read to them both and he was obviously pleased with what has been done so far, nodding frequently and whispering to Flo that that was exactly the way it happened. But he doesn't understand about the process, he says it is over his head, and he doesn't believe that part of it for a moment. He is nearly blind now in his right eye, deaf in the right ear except for a noise which he has complained about roaring in there for years, his gallbladder kicks up when he eats the wrong food, which he does frequently, and the slightest bit of stress, often, I suspect, the six o'clock news repeated again at eleven, gives him a pain in the chest and then he takes nitro and Valium to sleep. So my process concerns him far less than just seeing the book finished.

We talked about going to Volkovysk. He has wanted to do so for many years, not having been back since he left there in 1920. Flo has resisted, as she has resisted other trips, feeling that the worst would surely happen. Surprisingly, she gave in this time without an argument and agreed that the three of us might go in the spring. This was at the beginning of my stay when he was feeling well. He said then that he knew it would be a long and difficult journey, but that he was prepared for any eventuality. Whatever happened, he said, it was his decision and responsibility, no one else's.

But by the time I left he was not feeling well. He was weak and in pain. He took me aside and said that perhaps the trip would be too much for him after all.

"Some days I feel strong enough to lick the world, but a lot of the time I feel like this and I think: Who am I kidding? It would also cost a lot of money which we don't have. I'll have to think about it some more."

I told him it was all right either way, it was his decision and I would support him whatever he eventually decided. But I don't think we will go and I am disappointed. I too have an urge to see Volkovysk again.

My father continues dutifully to write his notes. His name is now Leonard. He loves his wife and he loves being married. He makes love "morning, noon, and night," but while his sex life has improved, his business life is deteriorating. The two clothing stores in Pennsylvania and West Virginia, of which he is a junior partner with his two brothers Max and Sam, are about to go under in 1925 as a result of prolonged strikes in the mines and a long list of impatient creditors.

Leonard's life is no less interesting and heartwarming than Lazar's, but for some reason I do not identify with the young man in America as I do with the boy in Volkovysk. It is as though the two are discontinuous. Lately I have had an urge to contact Lazar. I have no idea how I would do that, nor do I know what it is I wish to communicate to him. I will have to work both of those out. There is a diagram in Fred Hoyle's *Ten Faces of the Universe*[6] which describes a current event (or, as he calls it, "local system") being influenced by interaction from the universe coming from the future:

time increasing

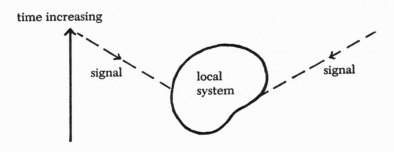

206

Hoyle speculates that consciousness may arise from this interaction with the future. I wonder if it works both ways?

Telepathy is the faster-than-light communication system that could facilitate contact between time frames (future — past). In action at a distance, the state of the agent's brain is said to affect the state of the subject's brain. Niniam Marshall's Hypothesis of Resonance suggests that the two substances exert an "eidopoic [sic] influence" on each other which tends to make them become more alike. What I am feeling right now is that Leonard in 1925 is my father at an earlier age, *but that Lazar in 1916 is my twin.*

The wind has finally stopped howling. The gulls still circle silently overhead. It is spring in Volkovysk and Lazar's life continues.

9. *It is a wonderful feeling to recognize the unity of a complex of appearances which, to direct sense experience, seem to be separate things.*—Albert Einstein, physicist [7]

In other words, all forms of time, including the chronological and the perceptual, are means of ordering actual events and measuring their relative duration. The notion that there is one unique universal order and measure of time is only an abstraction of thoughts built up in the limited domain of Newtonian mechanics.—David Bohm, physicist [8]

10. I decided to contact Lazar. Not "be" him, communicate with him, a two-way communication is what I had in mind. I don't know why. Perhaps to get his approval for all of this, or to prove something to myself, or maybe just to say hello, I don't know. It wouldn't go away.

I had no idea how to go about doing it. It would be a complete departure from the process I was using for the book, I was pretty sure of that. Still, after age-regressing to my own boyhood and finally locating the Kid (myself as a happy and fun-loving boy), I can call on him when I want to and we are able to communicate with each other. Why not with Lazar?

But how? Not three-dimensionally, I wouldn't be able to time-travel to Volkovysk and leave him a note. And I wouldn't want to frighten him or cause him to doubt his sanity either. The conversations with my father in Florida had been inconclusive. He could recall no unusual metaphysical incidents from that period—this would be between 1916 and 1920—no apparitions, presentiments, precognitions, not even an imaginary playmate or companion, nothing that would indicate his awareness that I had been there.

On the other hand, he could have forgotten, or he could have chalked it off at the time as coincidence, or we might even have agreed upon amnesia of the incident if there was one. I was, therefore, not dissuaded. It occurred to me that one of the most common forms of fourth-dimensional communication with which we are familiar is dreams. Maybe I could contact Lazar in his dreams. I wasn't sure how to go about attempting it, but that seemed the way to go.

About that time Theodore Barber was to be in San Francisco for a two-day workshop on hypnosis and we arranged to have dinner together his last night. At dinner I told Ted about the book and about my process for time traveling. He was fascinated. While he has always viewed age regression as highly imaginative recall and I was now describing it as time travel, he was receptive to the idea and said he would like to think about it and get back to me.

I told Barber about my desire to contact Lazar through his dreams and asked him if he had any ideas as to how I might attempt that. He suggested that I might put myself into a dream state just prior to attempting contact. I asked him to explain that further. He said he would think about that too and write to me. We left it at that.

3 January 1979
Dear my:

It was good to see you in San Francisco. Since I perceive every aspect of being in terms of levels, I do not see any necessary contradiction between "age regression" and "time travel." At one level, age regression to childhood or to a past life and age progression to the future involve a fantasied reconstruction or construction of past or future events utilizing whatever cues and experiences are available to us; at another level, however, these "fantasied constructions" may contact another level of being which is beyond our (lower-level) understanding.

208

I think you should try being Lazar in your/his dreams. Before going to sleep at night, or before napping during the day, set yourself (by self-suggestions and instructions) to be Lazar sleeping and dreaming. Specifically, during a half hour period when you are slowing down and preparing to go to bed, listen to a tape recording you have made for yourself telling yourself that (a) you are becoming very relaxed, calm, at peace, drowsy, sleepy, and ready to sleep and dream in a new way with new dimensions and (b) as you sleep and dream, your dream thoughts and the dream thoughts of Lazar will fuse, blend, and intertwine. Word the suggestions and instructions in your own way to speak to that part of you that creates dreams. Program your dream consciousness (by instructions and suggestions) to fuse with the dream consciousness of Lazar. Ask a bedmate to "arouse" you sufficiently at specified times while you are asleep in order to elicit your report of the ongoing dream.

I am sure you can program yourself prior to sleep to fuse your dream consciousness with that of Lazar. You should also be able to set up an arrangement where you are "partly aroused" at times during sleep so that you can report the dream(s) into a cassette tape recorder.

Let me know how this turns out.

> *Warm regards,*
> *Ted*[9]

11. *In the frequency domain, time and space become collapsed. In a sense, everything is happening all at once, synchronously. . . . While we don't know what the mechanisms for a leap to the paranormal may be, for the first time, we have to suspend our disbelief in such phenomena because there is now a scientific base that allows understanding. Perhaps if we could discover the rules for "tuning in" on the holographic implicate domain* [Bohm's Implicate Order] *we could come to some agreement as to what constitutes normal and paranormal, and even some deeper understanding of the implicate order of the universe.*—Karl Pribram, neurosurgeon and brain researcher[10]

12. From time to time I attempted to make contact with Lazar according to Barber's instructions, but without success. Usually I fell asleep before completing the half hour of preliminaries. I

209

would wake up every two hours during the night, often with dreams fresh in my mind but never one about Lazar, or else I would simply sleep through the night uneventfully.

There may have been something wrong with the procedure Barber was suggesting. Although I view dreams as out-of-body experience, I had never time-traveled to Volkovysk in my sleep, I had only done it while awake. I had also never before concerned myself to this degree with procedural details. Other than solitude and quiet relaxation, I set no criteria, I just did it and it always worked. It could also be that I was trying too hard and that the setup was too contrived.

Meanwhile, it was time for Lazar to leave for America and I was having great difficulty leaving with him. The details of the trip, particularly sailing from England, were very thin in the notes and I used that as an excuse to delay departure until I could check the facts. I read several books about North Atlantic crossings during that period, spoke to the Cunard Archives in Liverpool by phone, studied microfilm and microfiche of *The New York Times* and *The Times* of London and read the *Shipping News* for December 1920 and January 1921. I called my father at least a dozen times on one pretext or another.

As Lazar in the hayloft, I was filled with uncertainty, afraid to leave Volkovysk for America, afraid to stay because of the threat of arrest and imprisonment. I had little choice, I had to leave. I began work on the final pages. Everything went well until I got on the train. For some reason I was unable to continue the trip. The process I had been using no longer worked when I wanted it to. I could go to the hayloft whenever I wished. Again and again I made it through the back fields, waited until the last moment and ran to the train. But I couldn't go to Warsaw or Danzig or Liverpool or London, no matter how hard I tried. And I couldn't "be" Lazar on board the *Saxonia*. I didn't understand why.

I continued trying to contact Lazar. I focused on making the contact with him in the hayloft during his fitful sleep that last night. I did not succeed. I decided to give up on the attempt to contact him. For whatever reason, it wasn't working. I began to assemble these notes.

Two days ago, something happened without my even trying. I'm still not sure what it was. I went to sleep about one o'clock in the morning. I slept soundly until I awoke about six-thirty, refreshed and in a fine mood. The sun was rising, the sky was clear, there was a slight westerly breeze gently rocking the boat. I yawned, stretched, and became aware of a memory. I do not know whether it is the memory of a dream, but it does not seem so. I usually forget dreams rapidly. This memory remains complete, the scene is the same in every detail as it was two days ago.

I am standing face-to-face with Lazar. We are about three feet apart. There are no landmarks, no trees, no shrubbery, no buildings, just a flat plain. It is quite light, but there is no sun, no clouds, no wind, no horizon line. No words are spoken. Lazar looks at me with great curiosity. He is wondering who I am. I am conscious of his blue eyes staring at me very intently. I want to tell him who I am, but it doesn't seem important. I think he knows.

Then a curious thing happens. While Lazar and I remain standing exactly where we are, we also approach each other. We meet and embrace. Then we part. This is not something that I see when I visualize the scene. It is something I *know*. Then Lazar smiles, turns, and walks away. I smile back, turn and walk away too. I do not look back.

That's all. That's the memory I had two days ago. It is exactly the same today. When I remember the scene, I feel good. Peaceful. Very relaxed. I no longer have the urge to contact Lazar.

It may be that imagination is time travel, or it may be that time travel is imagination, or it may be both, or it may be neither.

13. *Defining usually means reducing a concept to other concepts.*—Hans Reichenbach, physicist, philosopher[11]

References to Notes
on Process

1. Arthur Koestler, *Janus* (New York: Random House, 1978).
2. Andrija Puharich, *Uri, a Journal of the Mystery of Uri Geller* (Garden City, N.Y.: Doubleday Anchor, 1974).
3. Jane Roberts, *Seth Speaks* (Englewood Cliffs, N.J.: Prentice-Hall, 1972).
4. Richard Swinburne, *Space and Time* (New York: St. Martin's Press, 1968).
5. Fred Hoyle, *October the First Is Too Late* (New York: Harper & Row, 1966).
6. Fred Hoyle, *Ten Faces of the Universe* (San Francisco: W. H. Freeman, 1976).
7. Albert Einstein, letter to Marcel Grossman, 14 April 1901.
8. David Bohm, *The Special Theory of Relativity* (New York: Benjamin, 1965).
9. Theodore Barber, letter to the author, 3 January 1979.
10. Karl Pribram, in an interview regarding his theory of a holographic universe, *Psychology Today*, February 1979.
11. Hans Reichenbach, *Philosophy of Space and Time* (New York: Dover, 1957).

DATE DUE
